"Rob Riemen *cares* deeply. About the moral and intellectual values in our fragile community. About that elusive but vital constituent 'decency of thought.' He is both a humanist in the classical vein and a shrewd observer of the technological changes at work in our political debates. To read him is to engage in a challenging exchange. It is to experience both anguish and hope—perhaps these two are somewhat mysteriously the same."

—*George Steiner*

"In 2010 Rob Riemen issued a warning that fascism could return. All that has happened since then has made this message more timely, as well as his recollections of loss of the humanistic tradition that underlay European civilization."

—*Francis Fukuyama*

"Rob Riemen's analysis of the reasons behind the current crisis of democracy and the rise of fascism is a remarkable document. It has the sharp focus and urgency that the sociopolitical moment requires."   —*Antonio Damasio*

"Riemen's book is a deeply felt and profoundly disturbing meditation on the sources and strength of the danger that European civilization now faces and an inspiration for those who are convinced that the survival of the European spirit remains within the power of the men and women who continue to view it as one of the world's noblest creations."

—*Anthony Kronman*

TO
FIGHT
AGAINST
THIS
AGE

TO
FIGHT
AGAINST
THIS
AGE

On Fascism and Humanism

ROB RIEMEN

W. W. NORTON & COMPANY
Independent Publishers Since 1923
New York | London

Copyright © 2018 by Rob Riemen
English translation of "The Eternal Return of Fascism"
copyright © 2018 by Rob Riemen
English translation of "The Return of Europa: Her Tears, Deeds,
and Dreams" copyright © 2018 by Rob Riemen

"The Eternal Return of Fascism" was originally published in Dutch as
"De eeuwige terugkeer van het fascisme." Copyright © 2010 by Rob Riemen
"The Return of Europa: Her Tears, Deeds, and Dreams" was originally pub-
lished in Dutch as "De terugkeer van Europa. Haar tranen, daden en dromen."
Copyright © 2015 by Rob Riemen
"Autumn Day," from *Translations from the Poetry of Rainer Maria Rilke* by Rainer
Maria Rilke, translated by M. D. Herter Norton. Copyright 1938 by
W. W. Norton & Company, Inc., renewed © 1966 by M. D. Herter Norton.
Used by permission of W. W. Norton & Company, Inc.

For information about permission to reproduce selections from this book,
write to Permissions, W. W. Norton & Company, Inc.,
500 Fifth Avenue, New York, NY 10110

For information about special discounts for bulk purchases, please contact
W. W. Norton Special Sales at specialsales@wwnorton.com or 800-233-4830

Manufacturing by Quad Graphics, Fairfield
Book design by Chris Welch
Production manager: Anna Oler

ISBN: 978-0-393-63586-7

W. W. Norton & Company, Inc.
500 Fifth Avenue, New York, N.Y. 10110
www.wwnorton.com

W. W. Norton & Company Ltd.
15 Carlisle Street, London W1D 3BS

1 2 3 4 5 6 7 8 9 0

For Eveline

Our age reminds one very much of the disintegration of the Greek state; everything continues and yet, there is no one who believes in it. An invisible bond that gives it validity, had vanished, and the whole age is simultaneously comic and tragic, tragic because it is perishing, comic because it continues.

—SØREN KIERKEGAARD, *EITHER/OR*

CONTENTS

TO
FIGHT
AGAINST
THIS
AGE

INTRODUCTION

In 2010 I published in my country, the Netherlands, an essay entitled "The Eternal Return of Fascism," at a time when it was already obvious to me that a fascist movement was on the rise again. If this could happen in an affluent welfare state like the Netherlands, I realized, the return of fascism in the twenty-first century could happen anywhere. The small book became an instant best seller despite the ferocious and angry criticism of the political and academic class. Their state of denial surprised me and still worries me—because I do agree with Arnold Toynbee when he, in his magnum opus *A Study of History,* argued that civilizations would fall, not because it was inevitable but because governing elites wouldn't respond adequately to changing circumstances or because they would focus only on their own interests.

Wise men like Confucius and Socrates knew that to be able to understand something, you had to call it by its proper name. The term *populism*, being the preferred description for a modern-day revolt of the masses, will not provide any meaningful understanding concerning that phenomenon. The late Judith Shklar, a renowned political theorist at Harvard University, was absolutely right when she wrote, at the end of *Men and Citizens*, her study on Rousseau's social theory, that *populism*

> is a very slipper term, even when applied to ideologies and political movements. Does it refer to anything more specific than a confused mixture of hostile attitudes? Is it simply an imprecise way of referring to all those who are neither clearly "left" nor "right"? Does the word not just cover all those who have been neglected by a historiography

that can allow no ideological possibilities other than conservative, liberal and socialist, and which oscillates between the pillars of "right" and "left" as if these were laws of nature? Is populism anything but a rebellion that has no visa to the capitals of conventional thought?

The use of the term *populist* is only one more way to cultivate the denial that the ghost of fascism is haunting our societies again and to deny the fact that liberal democracies have turned into their opposite: mass democracies deprived of the spirit of democracy. Why this denial?

One reason may be that from the perspective of science and technology, ghosts and spirits do not exist. Which of course is true—for Mother Nature. Human nature and human society are, however, a different species. Science and technology will never be able to provide us with a complete understanding of the human being with his instincts and desires, virtues and values, mind and spirit. Every serious scientist knows this. Alas, not that many in our ruling class do. Their understanding of society is limited by the scientific paradigm of proofs, data, theories, and definitions. The humanities and the arts are therefore ignored and dismissed. Yet the only knowledge that could provide a true understanding of the human heart, the perennial complexities of societies with their conflicting interests, the causes of modern-day movements and upheavals, and the real requirements of a democratic civilization is the wisdom of poetry and literature, philosophy and theology, the arts and history. This is the domain of culture; this is where we can find Clio, the Muse of history, always with a book in her hands, offering us the gift of historical awareness. But one has to read books to get to know her and benefit from her gifts.

A second reason the return of fascism and the loss of the democratic spirit are hard to accept is the embarrassment of the political left that embraces the tradition of the Enlightenment. The mindset around its "articles of faith"— human progress, the natural goodness of man, rationality, institutions, and political and social values as the main pillars of a just society—will always make it difficult to recognize the impact that the will to power, lust, desire, and self-interest have on the human condition. The point is, we human beings are as irrational as we can be rational, and fascism is the political cultivation of our worst irrational sentiments: resentment, hatred, xenophobia, lust for power, and fear!

Facing a fascist Europe, President Franklin Delano Roosevelt knew what he was talking about in March 1933 when he declared in his first inaugural address, "The only thing we have to fear . . . is fear itself!" He was well aware that societies in the grip of fear are responsive to the false promises of the fascist ideology and of autocratic leaders.

A sense of crisis, economic insecurity, and the threat of terror or war are the acknowledged causes of a climate of fear. The incompetence to prevent the return of fascism, to fight and eliminate it, is also due to an unacknowledged cause of fear and the main reason fascism can return so easily in mass democracies: *ignorance*. This is the third reason the denial of fascism prevails in our times. Acceptance of this fact includes the awareness that despite all our scientific and technological progress, the world-wide access to information and a provision of "higher education" for everybody who can afford it, the dominant force in our society is organized stupidity . . .

In my 2008 book *Nobility of Spirit: A Forgotten Ideal,* the final chapter "Be Brave" is devoted to the life of an exceptional man, a fighter against his time, Leone Ginzburg. A Russian Jew born in 1909, Ginzburg as a child emigrated with his family to Italy. He was a brilliant man who trans-lated the wonderful brick of a novel, Tolstoy's *Anna Karenina,* into Italian when he was just eighteen. Transmitting and making accessible the best of the European spirit—great literature—would become his strong passion. He translated, taught, founded a publishing house, and set up a magazine, *Cultura* (Culture), to do justice to the original meaning of the word: making room for the collection of the many roads people can travel in their search for the truth about themselves and human existence. Realizing that only culture can help people figure out the truth about their own lives and actions, he made transmitting European culture his life's work.

But then Mussolini and his fascists came into power in Italy. Mussolini insisted that all professors sign a declaration of loyalty—or lose their jobs. Of the eleven hundred professors, only ten (!) refused to sign. Leone Ginzburg was one of those ten. (Courage is a rare trait in the academic and intellectual world too.) He joined the resistance because he knew that culture and freedom cannot exist without each other. He also knew that fascism—which always crops up in the name of freedom—wants only to destroy freedom.

Ginzburg was arrested and deported. When Mussolini was overthrown, Ginzburg returned to Rome to fight against the Nazis who had taken over. He was arrested again and then tortured to death by the Nazis at the age of thirty-five. A letter he wrote from prison to his wife Natalia—it would turn out to be his last—ends as follows:

Don't worry too much about me. Just imagine that I am a prisoner of war; there are so many, particularly in this war, and the great

majority will return home. Let us hope that
I'm part of that majority, eh Natalia? I kiss
you again and again and again. Be brave.

I will never forget my silent amazement when
I read those words for the first time: *Be brave.*
What did he mean by that? I found the meaning of this farewell in Socrates, who taught that
courage is the ability to conquer not others but
yourself, the courage to be wise and just, the
courage to cultivate your soul. Whoever does not
do this is not free, and life without freedom, an
empty and accommodating life, is meaningless
and ultimately loveless.

Natalia Ginzburg knew this. She carried on
her husband's mission in his publishing house and
became a great writer of beautiful stories and
essays, including a short text in 1960 entitled *Le
piccole virtú* (*The Little Virtues*). The first two sen-
tences are as follows:

As far as the education of children is concerned, I think they should be taught not the
little virtues but the great ones. Not thrift but

generosity and an indifference to money; not caution but courage and a contempt for danger; not shrewdness but frankness and a love of truth; not tact but a love of one's neighbour and self-denial; not a desire for success but a desire to be and to know.

The cultivation of the little virtues, small-mindedness, trivia, kitsch, stupidity—what does this have to do with the return of fascism? Unfortunately everything. Late in life the director of *La Dolce Vita* and *Amarcord,* Federico Fellini, a close friend of Natalia Ginzburg, looked back at his own life, which included for a brief period being a member of the Italian fascist youth movement. He came to the following conclusion:

Fascism always arises from a provincial spirit, a lack of knowledge of real problems, and people's refusal—through laziness, prejudice, greed, or arrogance—to give their lives deeper meaning. Worse, they boast of their ignorance and pursue success for themselves or their group, through bragging, unsubstantiated claims, and a false display of good characteristics, instead of drawing from true ability, experience, or cultural reflection. Fascism cannot be fought if we don't recognize that it is nothing more than the stupid, pathetic, frustrated side of ourselves, of which we should be ashamed. To curb that part of ourselves, we need more than activism for an antifascist part, because latent fascism is hidden in all of us. It once gained a voice, authority, and trust, and it can do so again.

It is no coincidence that the return of a fascist movement is accompanied by the call to make country x, y or z "great again." It is the greatness of force, power, and the false promise of the return to an unattainable past. That "greatness" is the opposite of the great virtues that Natalia Ginzburg called for, and the human capacity to transcend ourselves, to have imagination and empathy, to live in truth, create beauty, and do justice. This is the true greatness of honoring the dignity of every human being. This is what a democratic civilization is all about.

To understand the meaning of big words, we are in need of stories. *The Return of Europa: Her Tears, Deeds, and Dreams* is such a story, about three big, often misunderstood words: *democracy, freedom,* and *civilization.* Their meaning matters more than ever as we are confronted with the high art of lying and the twisting of words' meanings, which is part of the nature of fascism. The return of fascism is always possible but never inevitable. Laws of history do not exist. It is the power of human freedom to go against the current and change the zeitgeist. That is what Friedrich Nietzsche wanted us to know when he wrote, in his *Untimely Meditation* "On the Uses and Disadvantages of History for Life," that we should not accept the blind power of the actual and that instead of conforming to the whole noisy sham-culture of our age, we have to be fighters against this age!

Leone Ginzburg fought this fight, and so did Natalia Ginzburg and many others who figure in the following essay and story. It is now upon us to fight against a zeitgeist that destroys the spirit of the democratic civilization.

I

THE ETERNAL
RETURN OF
FASCISM

All I have is a voice
To undo the folded lie

—W. H. AUDEN, "SEPTEMBER 1, 1939"

I

While the Second World War is ravaging the European continent, far away in the North African city of Oran, a doctor finds a dead rat on the landing one spring morning. He tells the concierge, and while he realizes that it is an unusual discovery, he doesn't pay much attention to it. This changes the next day, when he finds three dead rats. The concierge swears to him that it must be a boyish prank: "There are no rats in this house!" However, in the ensuing days, not only does the doctor come across more and more dead rats across the city, but a surprising number of patients in his practice suffer from the same symptoms—swellings, rashes, and delirium——leading to death within forty-eight hours. He knows that whatever this is, it is an epidemic. *Whatever it is?* A senior colleague admonishes him, "Come on, you know as well as I do what this is. What's more, we know that everyone, the authorities most of all, will deny the truth for as long as possible: 'This can't be true; we don't have anything like that anymore; we don't live in the Middle Ages; would you please stop panic-mongering.'"

But denial won't change the facts, and once the epidemic has the entire city in its grip, the phenomenon has to be named: the bubonic plague!

One variant of the phenomenon of denial is the idea that changing words will also change facts. Americans consider the word *problem* taboo. Any situation that would once have received this label is now called a "challenge." Problems don't exist, at least not in the United States of America. The word *fascism*, in so far as it relates to present-day politics, is likewise taboo in Europe. There is the far right, radical conservatism, populism, right-wing populism, but fascism——no, we don't have that: it can't be true, we don't have anything like that anymore, we live in a democracy, would you please stop panic-mongering and offending people!

In 1947, Albert Camus ended his novel *The Plague*—an allegory of fascism—with the comment that after the official announcement that the plague's reign of terror has ended, the doctor can't join in the mass celebration:

> He knew what those jubilant crowds did not know but could have learned from books— the plague bacillus never dies or disappears for good. It can bide its time for decades, slumbering in furniture and linen. It waits patiently in bedrooms, cellars, trunks, handkerchiefs, old papers. Perhaps the day will come when, for the affliction and instruction of humankind, the plague will rouse up its rats again and send them out to die in a happy city.

That same year the German novelist Thomas Mann wrote, "Nietzsche, like a sensitive stylus, signaled the arrival of the fascist era, the era we live in and which, despite the military victory, we will continue to live in for some time."

Camus and Mann certainly weren't the only ones who, once the war was over, quickly realized what we are all too eager to forget: that the fascist bacillus will always remain virulent in the body of mass democracy. Denying this fact or calling the bacillus something else will not make us resistant to it. The opposite is true. If we want to put up a good fight, we first have to admit that it has become active again in our social body and call it by its name: *fascism*. And fascism is never a challenge but always a major problem because it inevitably leads to despotism and to violence. Everything that carries with it these consequences is called a danger. Any policy that tries to deny a problem—or worse, a danger—is called an ostrich policy. It remains true that he who does not learn from history is condemned to repeat it.

II

Mussolini and Hitler—to limit ourselves to this demonic duo—became the most prominent representatives of the politicization of a mentality that had begun to develop on the European stage long before they appeared.

Goethe was one of the first to notice that a fundamental change was taking place in society. In 1812, he wrote to a friend:

> If you see how people in general, and young people in particular, don't only give themselves over to their passions and desires, but how at the same time the higher and better part of them is distorted and disfigured by the serious follies of the age so that everything that could lead to their salvation is doomed to fail, then you are not surprised by the heinous deeds which man enacts upon himself and others.

Soon afterward, in 1831, Alexis de Tocqueville discovered during his tour of America that democracy, beginning to flourish in a young country, was being threatened by a new form of repression never previously experienced in history:

> I myself seek in vain an expression that exactly reproduces the idea that I form of it for myself and that contains it; the old words *despotism* and *tyranny* are not suitable. The thing is new, therefore I must try to define it, since I cannot name it. I see an innumerable crowd of like and equal men who revolve on themselves without repose, procuring the small and vulgar pleasures with which they fill their souls. Each of them, withdrawn and apart, is like a stranger to the destiny of others. . . . Above these an immense tutelary power is elevated, which alone takes charge of assuring their enjoyments and watching over their fate. . . . It likes citizens to enjoy themselves provided they think only of enjoying themselves. . . . I have always believed that this sort of regulated, mild, and peaceful servitude, whose

picture I have just painted, could be combined better than one imagines with some of the external forms of freedom, and that it would not be impossible for it to be established in the very shadow of the sovereignty of the people.

What Tocqueville outlined here are the contours of a society that was analyzed and characterized by the Spanish philosopher José Ortega y Gasset, one hundred years later, as "mass society." Mass society is the inevitable result of what Nietzsche so lucidly predicted: the decline of moral values, nihilism. In the 1870s and '80s, Nietzsche became increasingly convinced that there was no longer any foundation for the European ideal of civilization, which was grounded in spiritual absolute values. There are no absolute values, he insisted, because everything that exists is nothing more than a projection of the human individual. Truth, Goodness, and Beauty do not exist. Anything considered to be such is no more than an individual's personal perception and interpretation. And anything that can mean anything means nothing at all, because it has lost its universal validity.

With the loss of spiritual values, not only did morals disappear but so did culture in the original meaning of the word: *cultura animi*, the "cultivation of the soul." The idea that man is a being who must elevate himself, who must rise above his instincts and physical needs, is central to the religious traditions of Judaism and Christianity. It is also integral to the humanistic teachings of Socrates and Spinoza. Only once we succeed in embodying our absolute spiritual goals are we worthy of life. Living in truth, doing what is right, creating beauty—only in these actions is man who he should be, only then will he be free. He who remains a slave to his desires, emotions, impulses, fears, and prejudices and does not know how to use his intellect cannot be free. Nietzsche inverted this, convinced as he was of the impending *Umwertung aller Werte* (revaluation of all values): nothing is absolute anymore except freedom, the freedom to live out your desires unbridled. Henceforth mankind will let itself be ruled by the will to power, and everything will be permitted.

Nietzsche knew exactly what the consequences of nihilism would be for European society. Later in life he wrote, "The danger of all dangers: nothing has meaning." With the loss of absolute spiritual values, everything to which man had attributed meaning would disappear: knowledge of good and evil, compassion, and the idea that love is stronger than death, but also all major art, courtesy, conversation, and appreciation of quality and of value. Hence his comment around the same time, "The most universal sign of the modern age: man has lost dignity in his own eyes to an incredible extent." Man, "freed" from all spiritual values and from being guided by anything that could make life meaningful, would primarily make things easier for himself. He would demand that all his desires be satisfied, and if that should not happen, he would become violent. This recurring threat of permanent aggression concealed beneath the surface of prosperity is something Nietzsche also pointed out in his notes of 1886–87:

Our situation: sensitivity increases with afflu-
ence; the most minor symptoms cause us to
suffer; our body is better protected, our soul
sicker. Equality, a comfortable life, freedom
of thought, but at the same time, hatred and
envy, the infuriation of needing to succeed,
the impatience of the present, the need for
luxury, the instability of the government, the
suffering from doubt and having to search.

Mass society is the name Ortega y Gasset gave
in 1930 to the society that, ever since Goethe's
first suspicions, has indeed manifested itself all
over Europe, with all the characteristics that
Tocqueville and Nietzsche predicted. And yet
Ortega y Gasset was amazed by what he saw as
the great paradox of the democratic age that had
just made its entry into European history. Here
you finally had an age in which society was able
to free itself from the yoke of tyranny and the
Church, aristocracy and the feudal system. Technological progress offered, among other things,
greater freedom of movement; the media broad-
ened people's outlook on the world; and politi-

cal government was increasingly democratic. Europe stood at the gateway of a free society in which borders could be demolished, individual freedom would be respected, personal responsibility would be assumed, and spiritual values that support the ideal of civilization would be cultivated.

But this historical opportunity was rejected by a new type of person who quickly won influence in society: the man of the crowd, the *mass-man*. The term refers not just to quantity but also to quality, to a certain mindset or, more accurately, to an absence of mind. Moreover, this mass-man appears in every rank or class, rich or poor, educated or not. According to Ortega y Gasset, the rise of the mass-man—the revolt of the masses!—is a direct threat to the values and ideals of liberal democracy and European humanism, traditions in which the spiritual and moral development of the free individual form the basis of a free and open society.

But the mass-man has a completely different outlook on the individual and on society. The mass-man does not want to be confronted, let alone burdened, with intellectual or spiritual values. No measure, value, or truth can be imposed on him that would restrict him. Life for mass-man must always be easy and abundant; he does not recognize the tragic nature of existence. Everything is permitted, for there are no constraints. Spiritual exertion is unnecessary. Mass-man is self-gratifying and behaves like a spoiled child. Listening, critically evaluating his own opinions, and behaving considerately toward others is not necessary. All this reinforces his feeling of power, his longing to control. Only he and his own kind matter; the rest should adapt. The mass-man, then, is always right and he needs no justification.

Unpracticed in—and not tempted to learn— the language of reason, he knows just one language, that of the body: violence. Anything different, anything irrelevant to himself, has no right to exist. He loathes being different from the masses. He conforms—he adjusts his appearance according to the dominant fashions and seeks his opinions in the warm bath of the mass media. At the same time, he does not want to and cannot stand out. The mass-man does not think. He wanders aimlessly through life, cut loose from any spiritual exertions, measures, or truths as guiding principles. Lacking spiritual guidance, he clings to the weight of the masses who lead him through life.

The twentieth-century phenomenon of mass behavior and mass hysteria are not a result of the multitude but a fundamental consequence of the psyche of this high modern, mindless, spiritless man. Fear and desire govern the behavior of the masses. And when these masses begin to govern, when democracy becomes mass democracy, democracy ceases to exist. At the end of his book *The Revolt of the Masses*, Ortega y Gasset summed up his analysis of mass society in one line: "It comes down to the fact that Europe no longer has any morals."

The nihilistic character of mass society is reinforced by a number of factors. In the first decade of the twentieth century, the Viennese satirist Karl Kraus slated journalists for tending—in spite of their pretensions—to undermine democracy more than to protect it. The pages had to be filled, newspapers had to be sold. The consequence was an endless deluge of trivia, sensationalism, and baloney. In the daily papers, Kraus argued, language was no longer the most important medium for expressing knowledge but rather had deteriorated into clichés, slogans, and propaganda. The mass media were the most important training ground for demagogues, and demagogues derived their power from the fact that the people, fed on an endless volley of simplifications, can understand only simplifications and want to read or hear nothing else.

One decade later, the French poet Paul Valéry analyzed the crisis of the human spirit. He stated that

> the spirit represents our capacity for transformation. Our emotional life can be transposed into works of art. The spirit creates new, intellectual needs, through which we can transcend our physical instincts and bestial natures. The spirit has allowed us an awareness of time, of past and future. With this we can look ahead, imagine possibili-

ties, and go beyond the present moment. In addition, a man can break free from himself, imagine himself in the place of others. Each person is thus equipped with the intellectual capacity to observe and criticize his own actions and values. But the human mind has become derailed. We have become less sensitive. The modern man needs noise, constant excitement; he wants to satisfy his needs. Since we have become ever more insensitive, we need more crass means to answer to our craving for stimulation. We have become addicted to events. If nothing happens one day we feel empty. "There's nothing in the papers," we note disappointedly. We have been poisoned by the idea that something *has to* happen; we are obsessed with speed and quantity. A boat can never be large enough, a car or plane never fast enough. The idea of the absolute superiority of large numbers— an idea of which the naivety and vulgarity is evident (I hope)—is one of the characteristics of the modern human being. We have forfeited our free time. I don't mean by this chronological time (our days off), but internal rest, being free of everything, the mental distance from the world we need to make room for the most delicate elements in our lives. We allow ourselves to be driven by speed, momentum—everything must happen now—and by impulses. Nothing is durable anymore. Farewell cathedral, built across three centuries; farewell masterpiece that required a lifetime of experience and attention to perfect. We live passively. We defer to telephones, our jobs, fashion. Life becomes ever more uniform. Appearance, character, everything needs to look like everything else, and the average always tends to descend to the lowest sort. One of the most striking characteristics of the contemporary world is its *superficiality*: we vacillate between superficiality and restlessness. We have the best toys that man has ever possessed. What a lot of fun! Never had so many toys! But what a lot of worries! Never had so much panic! And an ever increasing amount of intellectual exertion is asked of us. Others think for us. What's more, our intelligence becomes ever more specialized. Due to the demands of technological progress, society has a growing need for "professionals," *replaceable* intellectuals. There is no longer any use for a Shakespeare, a Bach, a Descartes, poets and thinkers, *irreplaceable* intellectuals.

This is what Paul Valéry wrote in the 1920s. Once again we are dealing with a paradox, because, in spite of social engineering, in spite of all the enticements and leisure, man has not become any happier. On the contrary, aggression toward other people is on the increase. This is logical, contended Max Scheler in his 1912 book *Das Ressentiment im Aufbau der Moralen (The Ressentiment in the Construction of Moralities).* European culture, according to Scheler, is a culture of equality; the idea that we are all equal and have equal rights is deep-rooted. In the Judeo-Christian tradition, equality consists of being equal before God: no matter who you are, no matter what you own, in the end you will be judged by God according to whether you have lived a righteous life. In the tenets of European humanism, the ideal of equality consists in the notion that our true identity is encapsulated not in the ways we differ from others (money, power, origin, race, sex) but precisely in what connects us to our fellow men: the universal capacity to elevate one's soul, to live in truth, to do what is right, to create beauty.

In the Jewish and Christian religions, as much as in the humanist tradition, equality is based on absolute spiritual values. But Nietzsche predicted that the meaning of these values would become lost. Equality could now be expressed only in the material. A new ideal of equality had arisen. It was connected to rising socialism and the drive toward greater democratization: social justice, equal opportunities, universal voting rights. However, Scheler suggested, when all values have become perverted under the influence of nihilism and the rise of mass-man and we no longer have any idea why social justice should exist, then the concept of equality will be nothing more than that everyone should be able to have everything and that what one person has, the other should have too. At the end of the day, we are all equal! *Elite* has become a term of abuse, and as soon as the idea occurs that other "equals" have more, resentment and rancor grow.

In this social culture, there is a constant drag toward the lowest point because that is where the population's common denominator is located. This is why the university education standard will plummet so that "everyone" can study— and graduate. As for the arts, they will have to be accessible to all, not only financially but also in terms of meaning: they will have to be *understandable*. The greatest rancor is directed toward anything difficult. Whatever cannot be immediately understood by all is difficult, therefore elitist, therefore antidemocratic. This is best understood in the world of the mass media. Here even quotations from thinkers, even difficult words, are taboo.

Scheler explained how a common culture steeped in resentment influences our values. Nietzsche demonstrated why higher spiritual values can no longer exist. Now an idea has come into play that these values don't have a *right* to exist, because they require effort and exclude anyone who is unable to summon the willpower to adhere to them. Instead of absolute values, there is subjective perception, with as its new highest standard "I can judge that myself!" This is how resentment also influences the ideal of freedom. In the Judeo-Christian tradition, freedom is the responsibility of every man to be what he should be: a righteous man. For Spinoza, freedom is the capacity to be free from stupidity, fear, and desire, and the strength to use one's power of reason and to live in truth. Only he who lives in this way and adopts the values that give truth to life—only this man is truly free. But again, this supposes that spiritual, universal values exist— and they don't anymore. This is why freedom can mean only that everything is permitted: indulge your instincts and desires. It is a freedom that will always be violent.

Like Nietzsche, Scheler understood that resentful people are ultimately weak and afraid of this freedom. The experience of absolute freedom will turn into a deep-seated *fear of free-*

dom, and the individual's need to conform to the masses will become enormous—the masses who ultimately want nothing more than to blindly believe in and follow a charismatic leader.

In this society, which is nihilistic because it is deprived of moral and cultural foundations, obsessed by the trivial and susceptible to demagoguery, and drenched in resentment and fear, politics becomes, as the Dutch cultural critic Menno ter Braak so appositely put it, "a matter for rabble-rousers, who know no other motive than the preservation and extension of their power. Power in the most vulgar sense of the word." Writing in the mid-1930s, ter Braak saw that a political movement was beginning to take control of Europe, a movement that did nothing other than exploit resentment. According to ter Braak, this movement was focused on stimulating aggression and anger. It was not actually interested in finding solutions, had no ideas of its own, and did not want to solve social problems, because injustice was necessary for maintaining an atmosphere of vilification and hatred.

These were its most important characteristics: vilification and hatred for their own sakes. Social resentment was vented on a scapegoat who was blamed for everything: the Jew. At the same time, this movement considered itself to be the eternal victim of the "left" or the "elite" and harbored a deep aversion to intellectuals, cosmopolitans, and anyone who was different. This political stand was fed not so much by stupidity, ter Braak said, as by semicivilization, recognizable in its continuous use of slogans and empty rhetoric. It was a reactionary form of politics that claimed that everything used to be better in the olden days and that it would improve again once its own people were cleansed of the alien elements that always ruined everything. Curiously but unmistakably, this movement cherished a firm belief in a leader who, as ter Braak observed, had never been proven a leader, but without him, his supporters believed the country had no future. This political movement had no real party program: following the leader was enough. The leader in question had to be necessarily populist in order to maintain his position; he put forward everything that would help increase his support and mobilize the masses.

Menno ter Braak set all of this down in 1937 in a short but brilliant essay entitled, "National Socialism as a Doctrine of Resentment." What he wrote in this essay about the attitudes of elites and intellectuals toward the rise of political fascism in the 1930s is remarkable. He was surprised that many members of the elite nonchalantly dismissed the rise of fascist politics: "Ah well, we don't belong to that bunch of losers," or "Once the economic situation improves, it will all blow over." *You are mistaken,* ter Braak responded, *because this bunch of losers represents the revolt of the masses, and where are you going to be when they take over?* Besides, social abuses and the economic crisis certainly influence the rise of fascism, but they are definitely not the cause of it. It is much too rooted in the cult of resentment and the void of mass society for that.

Ter Braak was not surprised by the role of the intellectuals, many of whom were themselves representatives of semicivilization: they might have read a lot of books, but their critical faculties had long since shut down. He was therefore not surprised that a number of them had become "infected with a certain kind of quasi-philosophical benevolence toward the supposed positive elements of National Socialism." He considered the intellectuals and scholars who said that more research was needed into the "background," "essence," and "essentials" of this new political movement to be more dangerous. They were wrong, ter Braak wrote, because fascism had no ideas, there was no profundity, even if the fascists would have us believe that it was a matter of "a revolution of the mind . . . without bloodshed." But the truth was,

It's all surface. There is nothing underneath. National Socialism is only knowable on the surface as a doctrine of pure rancor; these are recipes for hatred, intonations of envy, the shrill sound of slander. . . . The surface is all, betraying the fact that these aristocrats are perverted democrats, that these idealists of the masses use the "common man" for their own special purposes. . . . because what they so dearly desire is the unlimited expression of resentment using all possible means and any device that serves their goal.

III

The fact that fascism could gain political power in Italy and Germany was, to a great extent, a result of the hubris, as much as the cowardice and perfidy, of the social elites. Hubris is the overestimation of one's own powers, as seen in the Catholic Party and the German National People's Party when, in 1932, they were happy for Hitler and his henchmen to take over. They assumed they could keep him in check and use the mistakes he would make to politically eliminate him. Cowardice and perfidy like that of the German Social Democrats, yes: the opposition offered a vote of confidence for fear of losing even more favor with the voters. In fact, for all those voters who didn't vote for Hitler—the majority, *nota bene*—there wasn't a single party that wanted to lead the resistance to the

National Socialist monopoly. And this had everything to do with the deterioration of the elites,
who couldn't summon up the courage to stick to
their principles and social responsibilities.

The liberals no longer defended the freedom
principle of European humanism but became
interested only in the freedom of the markets:
that is to say, *As long as we can earn money . . .*
That the financial superpowers of the time simply supported the new political power was no
surprise. The Social Democrats renounced and
repudiated their right to exist when they stopped
preparing to fight for the cultural and moral
improvement of the populace and, focusing only
on material interests, actively encouraged resentment among the people. The conservatives were
prepared to unscrupulously exchange the pro-
tection of spiritual values for the preservation of
their own power, under the veils of "tradition"
and "social order." Among the intellectuals were
dandies and aesthetes who gawped in intense
admiration at the "pure aesthetics" that fascism
excelled in. Naturally, there were also reaction-
aries who had never had any faith in ideas like

democracy, social justice, or progress. Worse, they harbored such a deep grudge against anyone who did not dwell in their high towers of high culture that they were all too happy to believe in the "recovery of European values" that fascism promised.

This was how the fascists could come into power: idealess rabble-rousers with a politics full of hatred and resentment that was rooted in a fear of freedom and in the worst kind of small-mindedness. That fear could discharge itself only in violence, endless violence.

IV

We were supposed to learn the lessons of history.

Lesson 1. Primo Levi: "It took place in the teeth of all forecasts; it happened in Europe; incredibly, it happened that an entire civilized people, just issued from the fervid cultural flowering of Weimar, followed a buffoon whose figure today inspires laughter, and yet Adolf Hitler was obeyed and his praises were sung right up to the catastrophe. It happened, therefore it can happen again: this is the core of what we have to say."

Lesson 2. Theodor Adorno: "The only true counterforce to the phenomenon of Auschwitz is individual autonomy, the capacity for reflection, self-determination, not joining in, not assimilating, and being a man of character, an independent spirit instead of a characterless individual."

Lesson 3. Winston Churchill: "We must build a kind of United States of Europe, and we proclaim our resolve that the spiritual conception of Europe shall not die, that it shall live and shine."

Lesson 4. Thomas Mann: "No conference, technical measure, or juridical institution, nor even a world government, can possibly bring the new society a step closer if it is not preceded by a different spiritual climate, a new receptivity to the nobility of spirit."

Lesson 5. Albert Camus: "History may perhaps have an end: but our task is not to terminate it but to create it, in the image of what we henceforth know to be true. Is it possible eternally to reject injustice without ceasing to acclaim the nature of man and the beauty of the world? Our answer is yes. This ethic, at once unsubmissible and loyal, is in any event the only one that lights the way to a truly realistic revolution. In upholding beauty, we prepare the way for the day of regeneration when civilization will give first place—far ahead of the formal principle and degraded values of history—to this living virtue on which is founded the common dignity of man and the world he lives in."

V

We did not learn these lessons, and that is why they have already been forgotten. It is hardly surprising. Anyone with any knowledge of our cultural history, the history of the decline of values and the loss of the European spirit, who then considers our contemporary society, will be unable to avoid concluding that Camus and Mann were completely right when, as early as 1947, they stated that fascism was a political phenomenon that had not disappeared at the end of the war and that we could now describe as the politicization of the mentality of the rancorous mass-man. It is a form of politics used by demagogues whose only motive is to enforce and extend their own power, to which end they will exploit resentment, designate scapegoats, incite hatred, hide intellectual vacuity beneath raucous slogans and insults, and elevate political opportunism into an art form with their populism.

It is manifesting itself again. But just like on that spring day when the doctor discovers a dead rat, the next day three, and each day still more, when anybody with a sound mind and knowledge of things knows that this is a new outbreak of the plague only to collectively deny this obvious fact—now, in the same way, we can establish that what is obviously a revival of fascism in our society still can't simply be named:

"We are not fascists because we are a party for freedom!"
On October 3, 1940, Thomas Mann gave a lecture at Claremont College in Los Angeles on

"War and Democracy." At that time he had already spent seven years in exile because he couldn't live in Hitler's Germany. He had lived in Munich for more than thirty years and seen with his own eyes how a fascist movement came into power thanks in part to a complete command of falsehood: words were separated from their meanings and reduced to slogans. With his own eyes, he saw how first in cafés and in drawing rooms, then in the streets, and after that at mass gatherings, it was impressed upon the common people that there was a political movement and a leader for them: a man who was eager to devote his life to the needs, interests, and freedom of the common man, who would speak out and defend the values of the German people. And one of the reasons this leader was believed was because he didn't belong to the political establishment but was a true man of the people and spoke their language. On the basis of this experience, Mann warned his audience in America, "Let me tell you the whole truth: if ever fascism should come to America, it will come in the name of freedom."

"We are not fascist. Islam is fascist!"

Islam, like any other religion, has many faces. At its best, a religion will be liberating for its people, it will encourage them to love life by loving their neighbors, and it will encourage compassion, justice, clemency, hospitality, and respect for nature. At its worst, a religion is fundamentalist and totalitarian, subjugating people and robbing them of their freedom, and is intolerant. Islamists devote themselves to the pure, perfect—and therefore totalitarian—Islamic state, and in Iran fundamentalists have already put this into practice. The history of Christianity has also known episodes when apocalyptic visions and longings for a pure Christian world, a kingdom of God on earth, were used as justifications for crusades, religious wars, inquisitions, the burning of heretics and witches, the creation of ghettos, and hatred and anti-Semitism leading to the factories of death. Judaism also has its fundamentalists. All religions can become totalitarian, just as every ideology can be totalitarian. And any resistance to injustice or putative injustice can degenerate into terror and terrorism.

However, we must never forget that fascism has a preeminently *European* history. It has its roots in *our* culture of the mindless mass society. The factories of death were *here*, and here is where totalitarian terror and murder took place, during the course of which we welcomed these demagogues with open arms and then looked on apathetically. It was in this resentment-soaked society that a fear of freedom and a resistance to anything different was cultivated and is being cultivated once again.

"Islamization represents the greatest danger!"
The 2008 financial crisis has had far-reaching consequences for our prosperity. The globalizing economy, with China and India as its new superpowers, will also have major socioeconomic consequences. The worldwide environmental crisis can be catastrophic for the future of our planet. Our democracy finds itself in crisis. Political parties no longer have any vision; trust in politics and in public government has decreased to a dangerous level; elections are reduced to carnivals of trivia devoid of content.

There is unmistakably a deep cultural crisis in our society. We no longer know what our common spiritual values are, education no longer provides self-cultivation and moral training, and we no longer have any idea how to answer the fundamental questions which form the basis of every ideal of civilization: *What is the right way to live? What is a good society?*

What has Islam got to do with all these crises? Nothing. Within the European Islamic community, is there a serious political movement that attempts to "Islamize" Europe? No. Are there among the Muslims fanatics who greet anything that resembles criticism or that mocks what is sacred to them with passion and hullabaloo and are keen to respond to it with murder and terror? Yes. Are there Muslim fundamentalists who hate the West and would like to cleanse the whole world of infidels and everything un-Islamic? Certainly. But a far greater threat to our society than Islamic fundamentalism is the crisis inherent in mass society: the moral crisis, the ever-increasing trivialization and dumbing-down of our society. This civilization crisis is the true threat to our fundamental values, which we have to protect and maintain so that we can remain a *civilized* society. What's more, Islamic fundamentalism and terrorism will never be vanquished with European fascism.

"We aren't fascists because we are pro-Jewish!"

There are many good reasons to read Giorgio Bassani's wonderful 1962 novel *The Garden of the Finzi-Continis*. One of them is to learn that a number of faithful supporters of Mussolini were upper-middle-class Italian jews. On March 23, 1919, Mussolini founded his Fasci Italiani di Combattimento (which would later become the *Partito Nazionale Fascista*). Soon afterward Ettore Ovazza, the president of the Jewish community in Turin, joined the party. His belief in fascism was profound, and he defended it fiercely, for example, by setting up the newspaper *La nostra bandiera* (Our Flag) in which he disseminated fascist ideology on behalf of the Jews. Mussolini appreciated this. He didn't have a problem with Jews. His mistress was Jewish, and a member of his government was Jewish. Until late in the 1930s, *il Duce* loathed *der*

Führer. He proudly stated, "Fascism is a regime that is rooted in the great cultural traditions of the Italian people! That National Socialism is pure barbarism." And to Nahum Goldmann, one of the leaders of the World Jewish Congress, he avowed, "Hitler is an idiot, a fanatical rascal. When there is no trace of Hitler left, the Jews will still be a great people. We Italians and Jews are great historical powers. Herr Hitler is a joke."

You can never trust a fascist. When, in 1938, it suited *il Duce* better to keep on *der Führer*'s good side, race laws were introduced in Italy. Not even the Jewish fascists escaped death.

Fascism is not by definition anti-Semitic. Rather, it requires the delusion of the omnipresent "enemy." Being pro-Jewish or pro-Israel doesn't mean that you can't also be a fascist.

"We are upholders of Judeo-Christian and humanistic beliefs!"
This is another lie, a slogan for and by the semi-civilized who think they should find something to say about their *own culture.* Anyone actually adhering to Judeo-Christian and humanistic

beliefs will necessarily have learned this commandment: "And you shall also love the stranger, for you were strangers in the land of Egypt" (Deuteronomy 10:19).

The defender of Judeo-Christian and humanistic traditions will always believe in a universal ethics that includes all people. Our true identity is determined not by nationality, origin, language, belief, income, race, or any way in which people differ from one another, but precisely by what unites us and makes the unity of mankind possible: universal spiritual values that shape human dignity and that every man can adopt. Hence these traditions place education far above material interests and see life as a permanent exercise in knowing and adopting absolute values such as truth, justice, compassion, and beauty. These traditions place the arts, the classics, philosophy, and theology at the center of education because they are the most important set of instruments for coaching us in virtue and will help us acquire a certain wisdom.

The follower of one or all of these beliefs will do his utter best to resist a social culture of resentment, the designation of scapegoats just because they belong to a different faith or belief system, and all the hatred that this demagoguery incites. The follower of one of these beliefs will aim not to control the masses but to elevate the people.

The follower of one or all of these beliefs will adhere to the idea of the European spirit and will advance a political unification of Europe.

The follower of one or all of these beliefs knows the commandment: "Thou shalt not lie" (Leviticus 19:11).

Anyone who really wants to be a humanist rejects every form of fanaticism and learns the courtesy of the heart and the art of conversation, dialogue.

In the Netherlands, what the Party for Freedom (PVV, Partij voor de Vrijheid) actually offers is the shameless opposite of the Judeo-Christian and humanist traditions: vulgar materialism, oppressive nationalism, xenophobia, ammunition for resentment, a deep aversion to the arts and the exercise of spiritual values, a suffocating spiritual bigotry, a fierce resistance to the European spirit, and continuous lies as politics.

The most perverse example of the party's mendacity is the following comment in its political program. In the chapter "Opting for Our Culture," under the heading "Solutions," we read: "On May 4, we commemorate the victims of (National) Socialism. On May 5, we celebrate our liberation. This will remain so. May 5 will be an annual national holiday." It really does say "(National) Socialism"! Put the word *National* between parentheses, and the emphasis falls on . . . Socialism! Hitler was apparently a Socialist, and so the victims we commemorate on May 4 are actually the victims of Socialism, of the "Left" hated by the Party for Freedom. It is an indication of the PVV's true character: put the truth in parentheses, shamelessly twist facts, and lie continuously.

"Many intellectuals support us!"
Indeed. The intellectuals' betrayal is a timeless phenomenon. Conformism and political idiocy seem to be characteristics that many of our erudite friends share.

"More and more young people are voting for us!"

The children of this new world claim they have it tougher than we ever did because adventure, misery, absolute uncertainty is their lot, while we have been allowed to grow up in the economic security of the civil era. The point is, they no longer know about "civilization" in its highest and deepest sense, about working on one's self, about individual responsibility and effort. Instead, they collectively seek comfort. The collective is an idle sphere compared to the individual, idle to the point of debauchery; what the collectivist generation wishes, grants, and allows are eternal holidays of the I. What it wants, what it loves is intoxication. These young people, withdrawing from all seriousness in life, love to be swallowed up in the crowd for the sake of being swallowed up and don't care much for the objectives of the crowd's march. If asked to specify the happiness they find in this, they show little inclination to offer concrete interpretation. The I and its unburdened mass intoxication is a goal

in itself: the freeing of the I from thought,
in fact from all that is moral and reasonable;
and naturally from fear too, the fear of life
which drives you to join collectively, seeking
warmth together and singing very loudly. . . .
—Thomas Mann, *Achtung Europa,* 1938

*"We particularly support the people who don't
have it easy!"*
José Ortega y Gasset, Paul Valéry, and Thomas
Mann realized that European society would be
tested by a crisis of civilization caused by the loss
of spiritual values. They realized too that all other
signs of the crisis (economic crisis, the decline of
education and knowledge of the muses, increasing aggression and fear of freedom, crises of identity) are the result of this crisis of civilization.

In order to ascertain which form of politics can really address the needs of "the hard-
working people," a different question first has to
be asked: Has the twentieth-century civilization
crisis come to an end? A look at a random newspaper kiosk might help determine which values

we hold now and what we really find important. Such a kiosk at an airport or a train station is a microcosm, a reflection of the culture we live in, since you will find the same kinds of newspapers and magazines everywhere—they wouldn't be there if there weren't a large readership for them.

There is always a shelf for magazines on computers and other technological innovations, indicating our interest in technology and technological progress. Also standard is the shelf with magazines about fast cars, even faster motorbikes and motor racing, characteristic of our obsession with time and speed: the faster the better. The shelf for magazines with financial and economical information is unavoidable. Take one step to the side, and the photos of celebrities and idols smile back at us. They too are a phenomenon—it is no longer possible to imagine our society without them. And before we leave the kiosk, we pass the publications giving us the lowdown on lifestyle, beauty, and sex.

The next question is: Why does our society ascribe so much value to technology, speed, money, fame, titivation, and outward appearances? The answer can be found in something Socrates said in a conversation with friends twenty-five centuries ago: he criticized the kind of lifestyle that "focuses only on pleasure and ignores the highest good." This is the definition of a phenomenon that would become a concept only in the twentieth century, and then would begin an unstoppable march: kitsch. Our society is a kitsch society because it disregards the highest good, spiritual values, and we live our entire existence under the emblem of pleasure. The consequences are far-reaching.

Because there are no longer any absolute spiritual values, there is no objective measure for our actions, and everything becomes subjective. My particular I, my ego, becomes the measure of everything, and so the only thing that matters is what *I* feel, what *I* think. *I* insist that *my* taste, *my* opinion, and the way *I* am should be respected; otherwise *I* will be offended. The sensitive ego as a measure of all things won't put up with criticism and knows no self-criticism. Your identity is no longer an expression of your spiritual values (who you are) but of materiality: what you possess and what you look like. You can literally buy your identity, adapt it, and change it.

The constant compulsion to buy and possess is therefore not so much a manifestation of greed as a longing to have an identity that you can show off to as many people as possible in the hope and expectation that they will *like* you. Spiritual life is no longer relevant. It's all about feeling good. And you feel your best if everything is nice and therefore pleasant. Pleasant is the ultimate measure of everything you spend time on: your relationship should be pleasant, your friends too, and your studies and your work. You want to be entertained in your free time, and so mass media, sports, games, hobbies, and the arts have to be pleasant above all else. In the unlikely event that you don't feel good, and when changing your relationships or occupation won't help, popping a pill should soon take the unpleasant feeling away. Luckily these remedies can be purchased and are freely available.

When nothing is absolute, nothing is eternal either: everything is finite and transitory. This is why we no longer have any time or patience and why we are obsessed with speed and novelty. Here is the reason for our deep-seated fear of death, the constant need to be eternally young, the idolatry of youth, and its inherent infantilization.

In a kitsch society, politics is no longer a public arena for serious debate on what a good society is and how it can be achieved. It has become primarily a circus where people try to gain and hold on to political power with slogans and a public image. In this society, the economy is dominated by the spirit of commerce, which wants to earn money at the cost of everything else (people, environment, quality) and which requires anyone who falls under its spell to conform, to be competitive, productive, efficient, and commercial—above all, not oneself. Education is no longer intended as a process of character formation to help people live in truth and create beauty, carry out justice, and convey a certain wisdom. It has degenerated into an instrument for the transfer of everything useful, knowledge that is usable for the economy and everything you need to know in order to earn money.

Where kitsch reigns, nothing retains any

intrinsic value. Everything that exists is allowed to exist because it is considered useful and/or pleasurable. Kitsch is the irresistible temptation of the pleasant and the beautiful, but it is a beauty without truth. It is akin to a cosmetic that is used for seduction but also aims to conceal: the concealment of a fathomless spiritual void. Kitsch is the lie that suggests that a thing does have value and is important while in fact it is a constant flight from our own soul, which knows that appearances are deceptive. Hence the longing for complete oblivion: intoxication. But intoxication never lasts forever. Once it has worn off, life is no longer pleasant, and we are horrified to discover our own meaninglessness. This is when resentment, hatred, and rancor awaken in mass-man.

In May 1960, the Italian publisher Giangiacomo Feltrinelli wrote in a letter to the Russian poet Boris Pasternak, whose novel *Doctor Zhivago* he had published: "The 'fourth Reich' is the era of compromises, money, and intellectual poverty." In this single sentence he saliently encapsulated the betrayal of the social elites.

Nobody is born a mass-man. The opposite is

true. To become an adult is to become aware of life's great questions, primarily the question of meaning. But many people, especially those "who don't have it easy," are left high and dry in their search for answers to these questions and in their attempts to live freely and responsibly.

They are left high and dry by nihilistic intellectuals who maintain that humanism has had its day, that absolute truth and spiritual values don't exist, that nothing has any abiding value, and that universal, timeless values are history. In fact, everything is trivial, these sophists think—without realizing that they themselves are the most trivial of all.

People are left high and dry by conservative intellectuals who simply cannot understand that precisely because truth is absolute, we always have to be prepared for the changing shapes of truth through different periods, and that to be faithful to truth and to live in truth, we have to look out for the new, for change. We have to search for meaningful configurations if we are to avoid lapsing into obscurantism and going through life hardened and numb.

People are left high and dry by the education system. It has renounced the liberal learning in the arts and classics, an education that offered the spiritual and moral training through which one could grow from an individual into a person of character, and instead has moved entirely toward the dictates of what is useful for business and the state.

People are left high and dry by the business elite, who have the strongest influence in our capitalist democracy. They have poisoned society with the idea that earning a lot of money is the most important thing in life. By propagating the belief that "market value" is the absolute measure of what is important, this elite is responsible for undermining so much that represents immaterial worth and that doesn't bring in any money but whose upkeep actually costs money (the arts, our patrimony, care for vulnerable fellow humans).

People are left high and dry by both left- and right-wing political elites who have given up principles, visions, and ideals for the fake currency of voters' goodwill and of riding with the times.

Driven by expediency and unimaginative pragmatism, these folks offer populism. But populist politics is always deceptive because it is nothing more than the representation of the current fears and desires of mass society and its kitsch culture. This is why it won't solve anything; in the long term, it will only reinforce the crisis in its varying guises. You can hear it in the rhetoric of these politicians; everything they say is solely expressed in terms like *your money—our economy—our country—tough—security—social—antisocial—cost cutting—shortfall—tradition* . . . They hardly ever offer a real vision, or evidence an awareness that the essence of our crises is a crisis of civilization; that the economic crisis is de facto a moral crisis that won't be solved with more surveillance; that we will never be able to gauge or articulate our deepest experiences without the language of the muses; and that violence can be banished not with more laws or stronger punishments but only through the development of conscience.

They know nothing of the life of the mind or spiritual values. Here only power counts, a blind longing for power—which tolerates everything and refuses to see the rising fascism. It is through this betrayal of the elites that man becomes mass-man and his identity is reduced to that of a client, voter, viewer, or money-addict. Mass-man has fewer and fewer opportunities and receives less and less encouragement to be free and responsible as Socrates and Spinoza were free and responsible. Only by practicing the art of living, by mastering the virtues and spiritual values that dignify existence, can we develop a right-minded and loving character and be truly free. If populism in the kitsch culture of the mass-man becomes mixed with a large dose of nationalism, resentment, and hatred, we will see the false face of fascism coming to meet us. The rabble-rousers certainly won't solve anything for the people who don't have it easy. Fascism will just abuse them in its characteristic fashion: the lie rules.

"We aren't violent!"
A poisonous plant will first have to grow before it can sprout again and spread its poison. We are just at the beginning of contemporary fascism,

and it should be compared not to the fascism in World War II but to that at the time of its inception.

In 1935 the Italian Communist Palmiro Togliatti delivered his "Lectures on Fascism," an important document because this compatriot and contemporary of Mussolini was offering the first analysis of the new politics. He suggested that fascism would take on different forms in different countries because there were no ideas and no single universal value underlying fascism's credo. He pointed out that Mussolini was able to gain power democratically thanks to a social agenda that included voting rights for women. According to Togliatti, fascism had no totalitarian features in Italy originally and that in the early years of his power, Mussolini strove for coalition government. True, Mussolini had no qualms about allowing gangs of thugs to take on opposition leaders, making use of the militarized lifestyle after the Great War, but crucial to his success was the general belief at almost all levels of society that *il Duce*'s leadership qualities would bring safety, prosperity, and order to Italy.

National Socialism came into power democratically too, without ever being the largest party. The lack of moral integrity and particularly the conservatives' overestimation of their own powers allowed the National Socialists to gain power—which they then would never relinquish. They could not relinquish it, because the sole reason for their existence was power for power's sake and the harboring of resentment. Frustration leads to resentment, and resentment leads to violence, violence leads to more violence—ad infinitum.

This is what history teaches us, and unfortunately human nature has not changed. The institutions that should protect us exist only by grace of the trust that people have in them. Put demagogues and charlatans in charge, use the mass media to cultivate the belief that this leader, the antipolitical politician, is the only person who can save the country—and the constitutional, democratic institutions will disappear just as quickly as the authorities become impotent because no one believes in them anymore.

"We are antifascists!"

In 2004, the American historian and eminent specialist on fascism Robert O. Paxton published his impressive book *The Anatomy of Fascism*. In the twenty-first century, he pointed out, no fascist would willingly be called a "fascist." Fascists aren't that stupid, and it fits with their mastery of the skill of lying. Contemporary fascists are recognizable partly through what they say, but just as important is how they operate. Like Togliatti, Paxton stated that fascism, because of its distressing lack of ideas and its absence of universal values, would always take on the form and colors of its time and culture. Thus fascism in the United States would be religious and anti-black, in Western Europe it would be secular and anti-Islam, in Eastern Europe it would be Catholic or Orthodox and anti-Semitic.

But fascist techniques are identical everywhere: the presence of a charismatic leader; the use of populism to mobilize the masses; the designation of the base group as victims (of crises, of elites, or of foreigners); and the direction of all resentment toward an "enemy." Fascism has no need for a democratic party with members who are individually responsible; it needs an inspiring and authoritative leader who is believed to have superior instincts (making decisions that don't require supporting arguments), a faction leader who can be followed and obeyed by the masses. The context in which this form of politics can dominate is a crisis-tested mass society that hasn't learned the lessons of the twentieth century.

VI

In the Netherlands, Geert Wilders and his Party for Freedom are prototypes of contemporary fascism and as such are nothing other than the logical political consequences of a society that we are all responsible for. This contemporary fascism is once again the result of political parties that have renounced their own intellectual tradition, of intellectuals who have cultivated a pleasure-seeking nihilism, of universities not worthy of their description, of the greed of the business world, and of mass media that would rather be the people's ventriloquist than a critical mirror. These are the corrupted elites that have cultivated the spiritual vacuum in which fascism can grow large again.

VII

In 1951, four years after his novel *The Plague*, Albert Camus published his greatest essay, *L'homme révolté* (The Rebel), in which he examined European culture in order to ascertain why dehumanization could take place in Europe in particular. He wanted to know how so many educated people in a high civilization with so much technology and progress could knowingly wipe out the values that form the basis of our civilization's ideals. He gave us his answer on the last page: "The men of Europe no longer believe in the things that exist in the world and in the living man; the secret of Europe is that it no longer loves life."

It no longer loves life. This is the terrible secret of fascist politics and of the nihilist kitsch society in which it can blossom once again. Only once we rediscover our love for life and decide to devote ourselves to what truly gives life—truth, goodness, beauty, friendship, justice, compassion, and wisdom—only then, and not before, will we become resistant to the deadly bacillus called fascism.

II

THE RETURN OF EUROPA

Her Tears, Deeds, and Dreams

Whatever may have been the case in years gone by, the true use for the imaginative faculty of modern times is to give ultimate vivification to facts, to science, and to common lives, endowing them with the glows and glories and final illustriousness which belong to every real thing, and to real things only. Without that ultimate vivification—which the poet or other artist alone can give—reality would seem incomplete, and science, democracy, and life itself, finally in vain.

—WALT WHITMAN, *LEAVES OF GRASS*

I. Et in Arcadio Ego

Imagine: Europa, that beautiful Phoenician princess, who according to Greek tradition was seduced and abducted by the god Zeus in the guise of a bull and washed up half-drowned on the shores of Crete, where she became the proud mother and spiritual inspiration to a civilization of immense cultural richness. Imagine that she, Princess Europa, returns to that small part of the globe to which she gave her name because it was there that her culture and ideal of civilization first flourished. Returns, because she has been away. Far away. In the twentieth century: the wholesale annihilation of human beings, with entire peoples like the Jews and the Armenians uprooted; the destruction of her cultural heritage and her values. In the twenty-first century: a society that calls itself European but generally attributes the same amount of significance to her civilization and culture as to Egyptian civilization, with its death cult of pyramids and mummified pharaohs—interesting, even awe-inspiring, undoubtedly worth a visit and perhaps academic study, but aside from that not of our time and therefore not particularly important—from this Europe, the European spirit has gone. That was inevitable.

With some nostalgia, Princess Europa recalls how in Geneva in 1946, a number of right-minded intellectuals gathered to discuss the significance, the necessity, of *l'esprit européen* to the rebuilding of a ruined world. But even then she suspected that the number of listeners to speeches that were as erudite as they were passionate would be limited to the forty gathered in the musty conference hall. A similar skepticism took hold of Princess Europa when she heard about an initiative by several Jewish intellectuals and a publisher who had survived the Shoah, namely the publication of a new magazine, *European Judaism*. From the start, she believed the title expressed a wish that would never again be a reality. Princess Europa, with her civilization and culture, found herself banished to the realm of the past and its adjacent realm of oblivion.

Now imagine that this princess returns from exile. We have no idea by what means, but she's back. How should we imagine her return? She has no house, nor any fixed location. The princess will therefore walk into a hotel and introduce herself as . . . Europa! But that's where the problems start, because the friendly receptionist will ask to see her passport. She doesn't have one, can't have one, because she doesn't belong to any specific nationality. That is a problem, of course, but because the hotel is far from full, and the receptionist is far from insensitive to the young lady's mild expression and charming appearance, he kindly gives her to understand that if she really doesn't have any identity papers with her—"That's possible, madame, that's possible. It doesn't happen often but sometimes it does, and well, papers are merely papers. It's the human being that matters, isn't it? We all too often forget that. I'll put something together for our files"—he can nevertheless arrange for a room that needn't cost any more, including breakfast, than . . .

When Europa admits that she doesn't have any money on her either, the smile so firmly set upon the receptionist's face disappears, and he asks in amazement why, in that case, she's come to the hotel.

"But you already know," she answers with a smile. "I'm here for a room."

"With no money to pay for it," the receptionist says sternly. Then, looking as if he's suddenly understood something, his tone becomes friendlier: "You don't have a passport, nor any money. May I ask where you are actually from?"

Europa answers: "I was born long ago in Phoenicia, which is now called Lebanon. Since then I've been all over the world—"

"Now I understand," the receptionist interrupts. Then, his voice muted so that none of the guests in the lobby will hear: "I realize you're a refugee and I'd certainly help you if I could. But look, this is a hotel, not a refugee center, and you've got no money to pay for a room. I'm truly sorry, but we can't give you any further assistance here."

"My dear man, you're mistaken. I'm not a refugee. I'm more like a returned exile. At least," she adds mockingly, "I'm an exile who's trying to return to where her house ought to be. It's true that I don't have any money, but I wasn't aware it was going to be so important here. I do have something incomparable, something infinitely more important, something that's sorely lacking here." She answers the receptionist's quizzical look with a smile and quietly tells him, "I have a soul."

After Princess Europa says this, she disappears in a flash, leaving the receptionist dumbfounded. He can only think that he ought not to have drunk that half-bottle of white wine at lunch.

There is one hotel where Europa, should the princess indeed return, would be welcome even without any money: Grand Hotel Waldhaus, in

Sils-Maria, Switzerland. This occurred to me when a Swiss friend invited me to discuss a meeting to be organized as part of the Nietzsche Colloquium, held annually at Grand Hotel Waldhaus, on the subject "Nietzsche—Thomas Mann—The Future of Europe."

Grand Hotel Waldhaus. I was there once before, years ago. Sils-Maria, in the Swiss Alps of the Upper Engadine between two deep-blue mountain lakes, is one of the most beautiful places on earth. It was recognized as such by Marcel Proust, a man of great sensitivity to beauty, when he spent several weeks there in August 1893. In his first book, *Pleasures and Days* (1896), he told how greatly moved he was by the overwhelming beauty of Sils-Maria and its surroundings. He walks past a lake encircled by pine trees and snow-covered mountains. It's sunset, the water takes on all colors, and suddenly Proust sees one, two, five little butterflies bravely flying from bank to bank. At the sight of so much natural beauty, his eyes fill with tears.

Proust was not the first person to be enchanted by Sils-Maria, nor was he alone. In 1879—more or less by chance, since he had been planning to stay some miles away in St. Moritz—Friedrich Nietzsche visited the high valley with its little village for the first time. He immediately realized he had found his Arcadia. The pure mountain air, the silence broken only by birdsong and the murmur of the wind, the grandeur of nature and the hospitality of the local people, including the pastor with whom he got along well—all this brought Nietzsche peace in which, during long, lonely walks, he was able to bring order to the unbridled stream of thoughts in his head and entrust it to paper in a small, sparsely furnished house. Nietzsche spent seven summers in his Arcadia, and ever since, Sils-Maria has been inseparably linked with his name.

Nietzsche wanted to be a "good European" and certainly not a German. In that summer of 1881 in Sils-Maria, he began writing notes for a book that would become *The Gay Science*, in which he observed that

we are not nearly "German" enough, in the sense in which the word *German* is constantly being used nowadays, to advocate nationalism and race hatred and to be able to take pleasure in the national scabies of the heart and blood poisoning that now leads the nations of Europe to delimit and barricade themselves against each other as if it were a matter of quarantine. . . . We are, in one word—and let this be our word of honor!— *good Europeans*, the heirs of Europe, the rich, oversupplied, but also overly obligated heirs of thousands of years of European spirit.

Some years later, again in Sils-Maria, in the summer of 1886, he wrote in the foreword to the second volume of his *Human, All Too Human,* that he dared to entrust his books, which he characterized as "travel books," only to "you rare, most imperiled, most spiritual, most courageous men who have to be the conscience of the modern soul . . . you *good Europeans!*"

It is therefore no surprise to discover that Nietzsche is convinced it's precisely the greatest of minds who realize that a political unification of the European continent is inevitable.

In his *Beyond Good and Evil*, the first copies of which reached him during his stay in Sils-Maria, he wrote,

> Thanks to the morbid estrangement which the lunacy of nationality has produced and continues to produce between the peoples of Europe, thanks likewise to the short-sighted and hasty-handed politicians who are with its aid on top today and have not the slightest notion to what extent the politics of disintegration they pursue must necessarily be only *entr'acte*, an interlude—thanks to all this, and to much else that is altogether unmentionable today, the most unambiguous signs are now being overlooked, or arbitrarily and lyingly misinterpreted, that declare *that Europe wants to become one*. . . . I think of men such as Napoleon, Goethe, Beethoven, Stendhal, Heinrich Heine, Schopenhauer. . . . They are related, fundamentally related, in all the heights and depths of their needs: it is Europe, the one Europe, whose soul forces its way longingly up and out.

As if having heard the call of Nietzsche, "good Europeans" came to Sils-Maria in large numbers, most of them staying at Grand Hotel Waldhaus. Thomas Mann spent countless vacations there, both before and after his exile in America, and on the final occasion, in August 1954, he stayed for two whole weeks, during which, after breakfasting on his balcony, he corrected the proofs of his essay on Chekhov, read a great deal by and about Schiller for the final important lecture he would give a year later, and with a glass of vermouth in his hand, discussed world politics with his friend Hermann Hesse. Rainer Maria Rilke came, as did Albert Einstein, Marc Chagall, and Oscar Kokoschka, as well as musicians, many musicians: Bruno Walter, Clara Haskil, Otto Klemperer, Dinu Lipatti, Wilhelm Kempff, Yehudi Menuhin . . . Sils-Maria, and Grand Hotel Waldhaus in particular, became in the nineteenth and twentieth century the European Parnassus, abode of the greatest minds of Europe.

Naturally I accepted the invitation, partly in the hope and expectation of finding there she whom I so wanted to meet: Princess Europa.

Worthy of a princess, Grand Hotel Waldhaus presents new arrivals with a majestic sight. Towering above the village, up on a hill, it's more a *Schloss* than a house, with tall towers and battlements. From the front it looks out across Lake Silvaplana and from the back toward Piz Corvatsch, whose summit rises to more than three thousand meters. Inside is the marble staircase with its red carpet and the Blue Salon. No, nothing has changed. Afternoon tea is still served between four and six, when a trio plays music. The use of cell phones in the salons and dining room is strictly forbidden. On ordering a drink, there is no need to sign a bill; people know and trust one another.

The owner, who greets all his guests in person, inquires with interest after *Herr Doktor*—a form of address reserved for any balding middle-aged man wearing glasses, as if baldness and spectacles were bound to denote countless hours of reading and thinking—and it gives him great pleasure to be able to welcome Herr Doktor. When I tell of my plans for a colloquium on "Nietzsche—

Thomas Mann—The Future of Europe," he nods sympathetically. The host remarks: "Certainly, certainly, *wichtig*! The future of Europe . . . you will observe, here *is* Europe, the old, *real* Europe, here among us it has continued to live. Fortunately you're not the only one interested in it. You are fortunate. At the moment we have a small but *ganz interessante Gesellschaft*, discussing '*Ich träume Europa.*' But I don't wish to delay you, you've had a long journey. *Bitte.*"

He opens the door to my room, with the view of a lake that brought tears to Proust's eyes as he beheld all the splendor of nature. Indeed, in Grand Hotel Waldhaus nothing has changed, as if time has stood still. Anyone with any knowledge of European cultural history will easily be able to imagine, sipping from a glass of vermouth, that Thomas Mann and Hermann Hesse, or Clara Haskil and Dinu Lipatti, are still in residence. There is chamber music every evening, and I had the good fortune that for two evenings my favorite works, Haydn's string quartets, Opus 76, were performed. To create an even greater sense of nostalgia there were dinners on the theme

"*Speisen mit . . .* ," at which dishes were served that had once been enjoyed by famous figures including Wagner, Proust, Balzac, and Mann. Nietzsche was, of course, absent from the list. With his intestinal problems, he was continually on a diet, and meals such as his could not have attracted hotel guests.

Nostalgia. That's what it was. That was all Grand Hotel Waldhaus was, and it felt increasingly oppressive. Not that I couldn't enjoy the peace, the beauty, the music, and the many reminders of great European minds—on the contrary. But if the old Europe as cultivated here was the true Europe, then Europe would indeed never be anything more than a nostalgic memory. There would in fact be no future for Europe. So what, I asked myself, did that "*ganz interessante Gesellschaft*" dream about Europe?

The group I already encountered in the breakfast room numbered about thirty. They were mainly older ladies and gentlemen, but they included four young men dressed in suit and tie. The company as a whole gave the impression of living in the early twentieth century rather than in the twenty-first. They dined early, in order to withdraw at around eight to the Blue Salon with its Empire chandeliers, oak tables, and blue sofas.

On the evening when I had asked to attend a meeting because the subject was very close to my heart—"*kein Problem, herzlich Willkommen*"—the introductory address was to be given by a striking figure I'd already seen walking around the hotel but, since he always sat at his own table, hadn't associated with this company. On the business card he handed me when I introduced myself, I read "Prof. dr. dr. hc. A. M. Bummel." To judge by his clothing, a black suit with white collar, this professor served not just academia but also the Roman Catholic Church. His slim posture and narrow, handsome face with bright blue eyes made the learned priest look young, but his gray hair led me to suspect he was in reality over sixty.

The Europe of which he dreamed turned out to be nothing less than a return to . . . the Middle Ages! In contrast to what is generally assumed, he explained to us, the Middle Ages were a time not of darkness but of light, not merely an interval in our history but its pinnacle. A united Europe once existed, in the Middle Ages, in the form of Christendom. What followed was an echo of what Novalis, whom the speaker quoted regularly, wrote in 1799: "Those were beautiful, magnificent times, when Europe was a Christian land, when one Christianity dwelled on this civilized continent, and when one common interest joined the most distant provinces of this vast spiritual empire." Just as Novalis had followed up his call to the past with a really very one-sided description of all the supposed blessings of the Mother Church, her servant did not shrink from eulogizing his Church and faith as if there could be a united Europe again only after everyone found their way back to the Church. It seemed his reasoning had fallen on fertile ground, since it was met with much nodding approval.

His lecture took a remarkable turn when he began talking about "that cultivated aversion to Christianity sometimes found among Jews these days." The comment introduced an exposition on the subject of "anti-Semitism based on a mistaken understanding of anti-Judaism in the

New Testament of which, regrettably, countless sons of the Church have been guilty, but after remorse having been shown by the Church, it is now time for Judaism to forgive and to reconcile with Christianity." Moreover, the pious professor said, it is a mistake to think that God had died with Auschwitz. God had been in that hell too, but imprisoned along with the prisoners. In short, the Shoah could not be a reason for declining to restore Christendom to its place of honor in Europe or to see it as the force that would unite the continent as it had in the Middle Ages.

The speaker finished and acknowledged the warm applause with a genial smile. Taking advantage of the fact that I was seated at the back, close to the door, I quietly crept away, in urgent need of fresh air. It was a clear autumn evening, and above the silent valley I identified the evening star and the five stars of Cassiopeia. Taking a walk through the woods surrounding the Waldhaus, I came to a villa higher up, known in the village as Villa Larêt, once the home of Olga Spitzer, a French cousin of Otto Frank. In 1935 and 1936, Anne Frank, then six and seven, spent her holidays here. A girl from Sils-Maria with whom she often played, Tosca Nett, one year younger, is still alive today, in 2015, and she has in her possession a small vase Anne gave her in 1937, when she parted from her little Swiss friend with words Tosca would never forget: "This vase is for you. Keep it carefully, then you'll always think of me, and we'll be friends forever. Don't forget me!"

I wondered in just what the learned servant of his Church was actually learned, since I believed his entire line of reasoning testified to stupidity and tastelessness in equal measure. It was devoid of any real awareness of history, and it was bad theology, reminiscent of the religious nonsense spouted by the friends of Job. How much more sincerity, truth, and compassion could be found in that *cri de coeur*, that cry for justice by Ivan Karamazov, who cannot and will not accept the pain and torture inflicted on a single innocent child when her suffering and tears are glossed over and polished away with the supposed promise of heaven, of future harmony with God. "Too high a price is asked for harmony; it's beyond our means to pay so much to enter on it. And so I hasten to give back my entrance ticket, and if I am an honest man, I am bound to give it back as soon as possible. And that I am doing," Ivan tells his younger brother, a monk. "It's not God that I don't accept, Alyosha, only I most respectfully return Him the ticket."

I noticed that I'd become angry. Angry at the professorial poppycock I'd been forced to listen to for a full hour. Pious claptrap from, I suspected, an armchair scholar, the kind of aesthete who, infatuated by beauty, cannot see truth and looks away from social reality. But a European civilization, the return of Europa, would be impossible without truth and justice as the basis of our social order, without the humanism that has always been Europe's defining characteristic. In the Middle Ages, the era that the scholar in his black suit called, in that nasal voice, "a pinnacle," neither truth nor justice nor indeed humanism was at all widespread. His argument that a precondition for the future of European civilization is the restoration of the authority enjoyed by his Mother Church in the Middle

Ages is identical to the remark by the priest who meets K. at his cathedral in Kafka's *The Trial*: "You don't need to accept everything as true, you only have to accept it as necessary." To which K. rightly responds, "The lie made into the rule of the world."

Truth can be known only because of the meaning of words, for what are love, friendship, freedom, and justice if we don't know what the words mean? Where language has become meaningless, no truth can exist, and the lie rules. The professorial servant of the Church was unable or unwilling to recognize, let alone acknowledge, that partly because of the acts of "the sons of the Church" (his words), because of anti-Semitism, the pogroms, and the extermination camps, and also because of abuse of power and a lust for sensuality and dominance within that Mother Church, his own religious language with words like *God, Christendom, faith,* and *redemption* had become meaningless because implausible for many people; by using them, he only magnified their meaninglessness, instead of making his own language plausible again. That didn't interest him. His "faith," his "*schöne, glänzende Zeiten,*" were in his mind justified by aesthetics. It was a cult of beauty, but of beauty without truth: it was kitsch.

Someone who understood this better than anyone was the poet Paul Celan. He grew up in a German-speaking, Jewish-Hasidic environment in the Bukovina, Romania. At first the Nazis interned him and his family in a ghetto. Celan was twenty. Not long after that he was put to work in a camp, but before he left, he did all he could to persuade his parents to go into hiding and above all not to get on one of those trains. They refused to believe what he was saying. He never saw them again. Celan was a poet. He wrote in the language that killed his parents. How could words in that language—after so much deceitful usage and propaganda, after it had been an instrument of so much inhumanity and destruction—still be meaningful? The meaning of the words had been burned, Celan said, and he felt the weight of a responsibility to enable them to be true again and to talk about the unspeakable horror that had destroyed his father and mother so that what they had gone through would at least be known and palpable. In 1945, for them and for the millions like them who were killed in extermination camps, Celan wrote his poem *Death Fugue*. It could not be described as a beautiful poem, but a quiet beauty lies within it because every word is true.

In 1959 Celan came to Sils-Maria in the hope of meeting the man who had once remarked that "to write poetry after Auschwitz is barbaric," Theodor Adorno. They did not meet, because Adorno, who was indeed to be found at Grand Hotel Waldhaus almost every year, arrived only after Celan had left to return to Paris. There Celan wrote a curious fragment of prose with the title *Conversation in the Mountains*, which begins: "One evening, when the sun had set and not only the sun . . ." It can be read as a description of how Celan imagines the meeting with Adorno would have gone had they met in Sils Maria. He describes two Jews who attempt to understand each other but cannot and are therefore able only to engage in chatter.

They chat because the big words have become unpronounceable or meaningless.

———

O Mensch! Gib acht! This line, which begins the song at the end of Nietzsche's *Thus Spoke Zarathustra*, has been immortalized on a rock in Sils Maria at the spot where Nietzsche claimed to have received the "revelation" from his Zarathustra, the prophet of eternal return, the prophet of nihilism. The rock can be found at the end of the small Chasté peninsula in Lake Sils. In the year of Nietzsche's death, 1900, two of his admirers, both of them musicians, had the words of his "Night Song" carved into it.

O Mensch! Gib acht! It's no accident that the setting of Nietzsche's poem by Mahler in his third symphony—*Sehr langsam. Misterioso*—is almost identical to the way Wagner, in his *Rheingold*, has the earth goddess Erda warn the god Wotan of the curse of the gold ring.

O Mensch! Gib acht! They are ominous words of warning. Thomas Mann saw, read, and understood them. Paul Celan saw, read, and understood them. Nietzsche wrote them at the end of a book in which he unerringly set forth what the consequences would be for a world in which important words had become meaningless, where there was no longer any place for the great, meaningful story, where the European spirit had dissipated because all that remained was the complete meaninglessness of everything.

This is the "new gospel" that Nietzsche brought to us in the words of Zarathustra: God is dead; there is no truth; there is no morality; there is no good and evil; "thou shalt" has been replaced by "I want"; remain true to the earth, because only the transient exists; but everything will turn again—the eternal return; and therefore there is no goal, no meaning, there is no sense; there is only lust. Being human is what we need to overcome. Become an Übermensch, a Superman, and enjoy the destruction, for everything is equally pointless. Values are replaced by powers, and where powers dominate, numbers will take charge, and faith in quantity will replace the desire for quality. *O Mensch! Gib acht!*

The next morning a splendid autumn day dawned. In the early morning sun, the snowy peaks were brilliant white, and in the sunlight caressing the water of the lake, an infinitude of diamonds glittered. A golden eagle calmly glided high in the sky, as if aware of being raised far above the human world. There are few places on earth so beautiful as Sils-Maria, but for me, it was time to leave. I'd seen enough, which is to say: I saw that I had been mistaken.

The sun had set, and not only the sun, as Celan wrote. The next day, like today, the sun would shine again. It would then set but would eternally return. And the European spirit? Europa would not return. Not here at least, in Sils Maria and Grand Hotel Waldhaus. Not in an old Europe full of snobbery, conservatism, aestheticism, and nostalgia for the Middle Ages.

Culture is conservative because it retains all that is timeless and of spiritual value. Culture is also elitist because only the most excellent can be sufficiently timeless and valuable. Everything that claims to be culture but is not an expression of timeless spiritual values is not culture but fashion. Culture, however, is never purely conservative and elitist, because the essence of all culture is the unremitting quest to discover truth and give expression to it. Precisely because this truth is absolute, raised above time, we mortals have no power over it, and in our quest, we will always have to prepare for the changing shape of the truth, a result of changes through time. Culture therefore always means being open to the new, searching for new forms that can stand the test of time.

Conservatism, conversely, is all too often a lie—a lie made into the rule of the world! A lie because it is not focused on the search for truth, which entails remaining open to changes through time, but is instead exclusively interested in the cultivation of the old, of what already exists. In defending its own interests, conservatism forgets that culture is never purely "fine art," it is also the search for truth (philosophy) and the creation of a just society (which requires a politics that cannot be conservative, because social needs demand change). The step from conservatism to obscurantism and reactionary politics is far smaller than the adherents of conservatism would have us believe. There is a dangerous neighborliness between aestheticism and barbarism, as Walter Benjamin and Thomas Mann became all too aware as they watched the rise of National Socialism.

If Europa will not return to Sils-Maria, will she perhaps return to that other Swiss location famous in European literary history, Davos? Davos is in every sense the opposite of Sils-Maria, especially when, in January, the international business world, political elite, and media descend on it. Dynamic, topical, and future-oriented; global politics and climate change—all of it is there. As are the reverberations of empty words, grandiloquence, noise, an obsession with money and technology, the idolatry—Zarathustra's prophecy!—of the Big Number; the intellectual void, cultural illiteracy. No, if there is a place where the European spirit is not welcome and never will be, then it is Davos.

From my balcony, gazing upon all the beauty Sils-Maria has to offer on a glorious autumn day, I realized that Paul Valéry and George Steiner may have been right: the era of European civilization has passed; the cultural sun has set and will never rise again. I looked at my half-packed suitcase and the pile of books still on the desk. And in my head I heard a poem, a poem by Rilke:

AUTUMN DAY

Lord, it is time. The summer was very big.
Lay thy shadow on the sundials,
and on the meadows let the winds go loose.

Command the last fruits that they shall be full;
give them another two more southerly days,
urge them on to fulfillment and drive
the last sweetness into heavy wine.

Who has no house now, will build him one
     no more.
Who is alone now, long will so remain,
will wake, read, write long letters
and will in the avenues to and fro
restlessly wander, when the leaves are blowing.

—TRANSLATED BY M. D. HERTER NORTON

II. Diary Pages

Instead of returning to the lowlands, I decided that, now that I had the time, I would travel to another hotel, where I would feel more at home than at Grand Hotel Waldhaus, a place where I'd be able to write my "long letters" about the possibility or impossibility of the return of Europa and the future of the European ideal of civilization.

That other hotel, Schloss Waldersee, lies only two hundred kilometers to the northeast of Grand Hotel Waldhaus in a geographical sense, and historically both hotels date from the same period, the early twentieth century. Yet despite their proximity in space and time, Waldersee and Waldhaus are two quite different worlds. Waldhaus has always been an international, cosmopolitan place where artists, writers, and philosophers like to stay. Waldersee, by contrast, is more a sort of worldly monastery, visited in the past mainly by the German academic elite and the old German aristocracy.

Wolfgang Waldersee, the current owner of

the hotel, once told me the fascinating history of his name, explaining why he had never used the title *count,* had scrapped the nobiliary particle *von,* and had deliberately chosen to use his grandmother's surname rather than that of his grandfather Johannes.

Honesty compels me to inform the reader that in reality this hotel still bears the name his grandfather gave it, but for all kinds of reasons Wolfgang cannot change that, however much he might like to. For reasons I explain below, the code observed by his circle of friends is such that out of respect for Wolfgang, we should consistently use the name he would have liked to give the hotel: Waldersee.

The name, the family, and the hotel add up to a story that tells of the fatal collision between the German soul and the European spirit. In this respect, it's fitting that Schloss Waldersee is located at the heart of "*Magic Mountain* land," the area of southern Germany where Thomas Mann wrote his awe-inspiring novel *The Magic Mountain* in the years before 1933 and that also forms the backdrop to *Doctor Faustus*, a gripping, largely autobiographical narrative about how the German soul, by arrogantly rejecting a European spirit, was transformed from an angel into a devil.

The story of Schloss Waldersee began with Grandpa Johannes, a brilliant Protestant theologian who wanted not only to write books but to evangelize the world by offering people a place, his *Schloss,* his castle, where they could be united "with the breath of creation." In practice, this esoteric ideal amounted to a belief that you must strive to forget your own ego, no longer think about yourself, and instead be absorbed into the great whole, the community of God. That, according to Wolfgang, was characteristic of the cultural Protestantism of the nineteenth century and the first half of the twentieth: "*Ich bin nichts, das Volk ist alles.*"

In Waldersee, this idea was put into practice fairly innocently in the form of a great deal of communal singing, dancing, and listening to music. But far less innocent were the social implications: you were expected to adjust to the God-given social order and to be neither critical nor materialistic. Jews were excluded from the academic milieu as by nature too assertive, too self-assured, too nonconformist and materialistic. According to Wolfgang, this cultural Protestantism is one of the reasons why as early as 1933, 70 percent of the Protestant elite in Germany belonged to the National Socialist party. His grandfather was not an anti-Semite, sooner a philo-Semite, nor was he ever a member of the Nazi party. Nonetheless, the God-fearing man was convinced that the Führer had been sought out by God himself and, as a consequence, must be followed. This combination of cultivating your inner self and ignoring as far as possible the sociopolitical reality, of being obedient and always adapting yourself to the interests of society as prescribed by the competent authorities, along with a firm belief in the moral and cultural superiority of the German people and their *Kultur,* is the poisonous mixture that, like a magic potion, caused many millions, enraptured and intoxicated, to embrace Nazi totalitarianism.

As Wolfgang was telling me this, I found myself thinking about the life story of Thomas

Mann, who until the First World War shared this typically Wagnerian worldview but then, confronted with postwar violence and disastrous reactionary politics, learned a lesson he would never forget: culture and politics must never be separated; and the creation of beauty is impossible without the search for truth and the pursuit of justice, otherwise beauty becomes a blinding lie. Or as he summed it up in a diary entry of May 1921: "Conversation about the problem of German culture. Humanism not German but indispensable." Only then did Mann become a European, only then could *The Magic Mountain* grow to become an epic about the European spirit, and only then did he understand why Goethe, Schiller, Heine, and Nietzsche wanted to be not Germans but Europeans.

That insight came to Grandfather Johannes too late. With the Second World War his worldview collapsed, and he died in 1949, utterly disappointed in himself.

Until 1951, the American army used the hotel as a sanatorium for survivors of the Shoah. But when the Americans were finally able to leave

Germany, the Waldersee family retook possession of it. What followed is worthy of a soap
opera. Wolfgang fled and managed to make a fortune in the world of technology, in the United
States among other places. In the late 1990s the
hotel came close to bankruptcy. His father, tired
of all the quarrels and financial worries, asked
his son to save the family property and make it
once more what it ought to be: a place to rest, to
think, to read, and to recover from the burdens
of life. For my part, I think the father hoped his
son would also help the hotel recover from the
burden of German history.

Wolfgang sold his business, bought the hotel,
and created space for a spirit other than the German soul. The programs of song and dance were
scrapped, and jazz was welcomed instead. He
built two libraries in the hotel and established a
small but well-stocked bookshop. Most important of all to him were the international symposia he resolved to organize, since he was seeking
answers to the questions that tormented him:
Why was the German intelligentsia so recep-
tive to Nazism? Why was it specifically the Jews

in Germany who became the object of so much hatred? What place will be given to Islam on the European continent? What is the ethics of technology? Partly because of his unease about what he regards as still dominant anti-Americanism and anti-Semitism in the "better circles" in Germany, he often invites American and Israeli speakers, with the result that in Germany's academic world, his symposia are spoken of rather condescendingly by people who are nevertheless more than happy to attend.

When I rang Wolfgang to inquire whether he had room at his inn for a few days, it turned out I was "more than welcome." He told me my call was serendipitous, since the next day a three-day symposium was to begin on the subject "What's Left for the West?" One of the speakers had just canceled, and I would make a great replacement, he said, sounding so confident, it was almost impossible to say no. To my question as to the purpose of the gathering he answered, "Now that the era of Pax Americana seems to be over, a hundred years after European hegemony ended, we have to ask ourselves what the West, our society, still actually has to offer the world." Over the coming three days he wished to investigate three phenomena that were Western in origin: What the West had to offer the world in the fields of science and technology, democracy, and European culture.

The task that fell to me would be to get the discussion going on the second day, with some introductory remarks about the place and significance of democracy. With "the return of Europa" in mind, I'd have preferred to be the one to speak on the final day, about the significance of European culture, but for that day Wolfgang had already found a Czech professor, whose name meant nothing to me, and I also had various ideas of my own about the fate of Western democracy, so I said yes.

When I saw Schloss Waldersee down in the valley a few hours later, surrounded by the Bavarian Alps, I realized that the symposium would not leave me with much time to comply with Rilke's encouragement to "wake, read, write long letters." But who could say what the meeting might teach me? In actual fact, the subject of Wolfgang's symposium was quite closely related to my own questions.

In the evening, a dinner was held for participants in the symposium, a group some twenty strong. I was pleasantly surprised to find two people I knew, aside from Wolfgang. Walter was there, a brilliant Austrian intellectual who prior to retirement had been in charge of the famous Brenner Archive in Innsbruck, where among other things he was responsible for the legacy of the publisher of the magazine *Brenner*, Ludwig von Ficker, as well as certain works by Ludwig Wittgenstein, Karl Kraus, and the now-almost-forgotten poet Georg Trakl. Walter knows this intellectual world better than anyone, and the same applies to the work of Kierkegaard, of whom he is a great admirer.

The other surprise was the presence of my old friend Jossi, a Talmud expert from Jerusalem who happened to be on holiday for two weeks in Waldersee and was attending the symposium out of curiosity. Wolfgang introduced me to the two other speakers: Shashi, an Indian American, not yet forty, who worked in California and was due to talk about the significance of science and technology; and the far older (I judged him to be at least eighty) Radim, the Czech professor. Wolfgang could not resist telling me that Radim had been a good friend of Václav Havel. The remainder of the company was made up mainly of people who worked for the German Marshall Fund, a think tank for transatlantic relations based in Washington, D.C. There were some German and Swiss academics as well, and a few international students.

Instead of letters, I wrote in my diary over the days that followed. It soon became clear that the subjects discussed had everything to do with my own quest for Princess Europa and her ideal of civilization. The greatest surprise was the contribution by the elderly Czech on the final day. But for the sake of completeness I'll refer to my notes on all three days of discussion on the subject "What's Left for the West?"

Thursday
After the sunny autumn days in Sils-Maria, and the still-fine weather when I arrived here at

Schloss Waldersee yesterday, it was a shame to see on waking that the entire castle was swathed in one great low dark cloud. You could hear the bells of cows or sheep walking nearby, but they were impossible to make out in the gray fog. At ten o'clock everyone was sitting in the library at tables that had been placed in a square.

After words of welcome from Wolfgang came the introduction by Shashi about "the greatest gift to the world: science and technology." The majority of the group, especially the Americans, responded with enthusiasm to his thirty-minute presentation. I felt rather disappointed, however, since I'd heard nothing new. Walter was visibly irritated, and his response made a far greater impression on me. The Czech seemed completely absent, as if not even hearing what was being said. He sat staring at a book, making a few notes. The enthusiasm with which Shashi spoke was striking, certainly, but it fit his message that "science and technology, *true* solutions, have now replaced philosophy and religion with their *true* knowledge." He went far further than those "true solutions," to present an entirely new religion that would deliver humanity from its vale of tears. The era of religions was over, an advance due entirely to science and technology. His quotation from Richard Dawkins was as funny as it was simplistic; Dawkins once characterized "the God of the Old Testament" as "arguably the most unpleasant character in all fiction: jealous and proud of it; a petty, unjust, unforgiving control freak; a vindictive, bloodthirsty ethnic cleanser; a misogynistic, homophobic, racist, infanticidal, genocidal, filicidal, pestilential, megalomaniacal, sadomasochistic, capriciously malevolent bully."

Shashi's assertion that it was far from coincidental that "Judaism and Christianity belong more to the East—where they come from—than to the West" was absurd. He was right, though, when he explained the degree to which science—and because of science, technology—came to fruition in the West at the time of the Enlightenment. All the good in the world was from that moment on attributable to this particular development; all reversion to barbarism the consequence of religion and irrational sentiments.

Here Walter interrupted him to ask whether

Shashi really was of the opinion that the world of technology was innocent of the industrial mass murder of the Shoah. Shashi calmly answered that technology and science are not responsible for the uses to which they are put. But soon he was contradicting himself on that point. He turned out to be a firm adherent of techno-evangelist Ray Kurzweil, a man deeply convinced that the *exponential* (a word that for his followers represents magical forces) growth of technology makes possible a fusion between IT and human beings. As far as Kurzweil and Co. are concerned, it will be possible in the not too distant future to make a human—or rather to create a merger that might be called a "human-machine"—that will not only be able to do everything faster and better but will be immortal as well, because technology will have taken over the body.

Walter remarked, mockingly, "I proclaim the Übermensch."

Shashi, and he was serious, said, "Yes, I proclaim to you Good News."

Someone asked whether humanity wouldn't

thereby be transformed into a collection of robots, and Shashi replied: "No, a robot is a machine with human qualities, but *the singular man*, the perfect fusion of man and technology, is still a human being, only with the qualities of a robot."

Instead of explaining the difference—which escapes me—he added threateningly that "we simply have to adjust to the fact that this is the future, these are the coming technological developments, you can't stop them, no one can. This is the new world."

Walter said then, "You mean *brave* new world." But Shashi did not respond.

I found all this irritating. First science and technology were absolved when it came to their role in the ultimate barbarism, now suddenly technological possibilities were equated with a natural law there was no means of escaping. This is to fail to appreciate the essence of being human, or at least of mankind as understood in European humanism: humanity is *free*. We can make choices. This is the very essence of having morality, of the knowledge of good and evil. The fact that human nature contains a great deal of aggression and that we are all capable of murder, looting, and rape does not mean we have to accept such aggression, that we simply need to get used to it, that it's just the way things are, and we can't escape it. Civilization is precisely the human capacity to say no, and it seems to me, we can also say no to cloning and to that horrific human-machine in the form of the singular man. I still find it astonishing that the techno-evangelists boast they are offering humanity a kind of eternal "progress," yet as soon as ethical questions arise, they lapse into complete determinism and fatalism.

Shashi's Good News was not over yet. All the problems of the world would be solved by everything that was smart, innovative, entrepreneurial, or a start-up. Over the past fifty years, he said, almost with a sneer, Europe has not managed to make a single real contribution to the new thinking, to innovative thinking. Everything that is now changing the world comes from the west of the West, from California. That is the cradle of the new civilization. Why? "We think positively and know how to *fix* things."

I believe Wolfgang was sincere when he thanked Shashi for his "truly inspiring contribution." In that sense, Wolfgang is a bit of a divided soul. His love for European culture is great and genuine, but at the same time he is completely under the spell of Shashi's vision of the future, which I cannot see as anything other than a technological "brave new world."

I was interested to see how Walter would react. During Shashi's lecture he had busily made notes, and from his body language, I could tell that he would be happy to see this turn into a verbal boxing match. With his heavy German accent, he said, "The West, and first of all we in Europe, have given the world science and technology. Another gift is even older, philosophy. Well, philosophy can't fix anything"—and he pronounced the word *fix* as if it caused a bad taste in his mouth—"but it can give us insights. Such as the insight that Wittgenstein, who was a philosopher and an engineer and an architect, gives us when he notes, at the end of his *Tractatus Logico-Philosophicus*, 'We feel that even when all possible scientific questions have been answered, the problems of life remain completely untouched.' Please give some thought to what Wittgenstein wishes us to understand."

Walter said nothing for a moment, so everyone had to think about the philosopher's assertion. Then he went on: "I have no idea what our young friends in California can or cannot fix, but being a little older than these new thinkers and perhaps in possession of rather more experience, I venture to suggest that the great questions of life, questions about tragedy, suffering, true happiness, and the meaning of our lives, will never be fixed by science or technology. Wittgenstein is right: science and the mystery of life are two different worlds. Of course science and technology are impressive, the fruits of great fortitude of mind and in many respects a blessing to humanity. Without medical science, I, an old man now, would not be sitting here. But you must understand that scientific thinking has also brought us a Pandora's box. And no, I'm not referring to the destruction that technology can also bring. I'm not talking about technology. I mean something more fundamental, something that encroaches far further upon our lives, our world, without our being aware of it."

Again that silence, that glance around, a sip of his coffee, which must have been cold by this point. Everyone was silent. Somehow or other Walter was making more of an impression with the calm tone in which he spoke, so differently from Shashi, on the subject.

Walter went on, almost in a whisper: "Science has deprived us of the truth."

Incredulous looks fell to him, and Shashi could not suppress a laugh—you could almost hear him thinking, *I knew it! This old man is a fool.*

Then came Walter's voice again: "You laugh, and I understand that, I understand it perfectly well. It does sound crazy. Science, science that wants purely and simply to enable us to know the truth, for which nothing can exist other than truth—how can science have deprived us of the truth?! Yet it is so. That's what Wittgenstein wanted us to understand, but unfortunately only a few people have understood it.

"You've heard a talk, and I don't want to give another talk, and yet, *Verzeihung bitte, es ist wichtig*, this is really important. Scientific truth is never more than reality, the facts, that which we can see, touch, and calculate. It is reason, rational, but reason can never determine value, it has no meaning. Reason can describe, it can inform us about the facts, but it cannot tell us what the moral significance of those facts is, because it does not know what good is or what evil is.

"Science, and this is its greatest gift, enables us to know *nature* but not the *spirit*. Science has to work with theories and definitions, but the human spirit cannot be captured in theories and definitions, and neither can our moral order, the recognition of what is or is not a just society. That knowledge belongs to a different truth, a truth that science cannot know because it's a *meta*physical truth. Perhaps out of envy prompted by the fact that there is another, higher truth, science has tried to deprive us of that truth, to make us forget it, to make us believe that everything that exists is scientific, has to be scientific, otherwise it's not important.

"A lie, ladies and gentlemen. A big, dangerous lie! A lie that unfortunately we've all come to believe and to which we submit. For us only facts count; we have fallen in love with data and information, and because we can no longer know true meaning, the only value we still recognize is economic value: How much can we charge for it? How much will it render up? And so everything has to be useful, instrumental, we 'have to be able to do something with it,' because otherwise it's of no use to us.

"Science has become an ideology, an idea, a delusion, in which we are trapped. Trapped because in our world only material things exist, everything has become money, everything is calculable and reduced to a number. Do you understand that? Do you understand the consequences, the terrible outcome of the fact that with the disappearance of metaphysical reality, we have lost all qualities, the quality of life, because quality is the expression of a spiritual value, a value we no longer recognize, no longer wish to recognize?

"The world, the future, as we have just been told, is becoming 'exponential.' Technological developments, data—it will all increase exponentially and change the world. Certainly. But do you know what else will increase ex-po-nen-tially? Stupidity! Science offers us knowledge, but not the slightest self-knowledge. Pascal, who, don't forget, was a mathematician, was right: *Le coeur a ses raisons que la raison ne connaît point.* 'The heart has its reasons that reason does not know.' The new knowledge, with the help of scientific knowledge, wants to make everything smart.

"But wisdom is no longer sought and science will never find it. All of higher education has to be scientific, which is to say full of theories, def-initions, and proof. Yet real literature, history, philosophy, and theology know no theories, defi-nitions, or proof. They tell stories, stories about being human, about human shortcomings and who we as people ought to be. Their truth is not scientific, because the truth they offer is meta-physical truth, which has been taken from us and is no longer taught. Who these days teaches how to read life?

"All this has made us blind to everything that is truly important in life and makes life worth liv-ing. Because what do we still regard as important? Utility, especially economic utility. Our ideal of knowledge, the world of culture, our social life—everything and everyone is measured by this economic yardstick. Economists have therefore become the new high priests of our age, who in an oracular language of theories and numbers declare what does or does not have economic usefulness, what must or must not be allowed to exist.

"Because quality of life cannot prove itself economically or scientifically, economics recognizes only quantity; everything is a number, so the economy always has to grow, because a larger number is better than a smaller number, whatever the social consequences. All that counts is money. 'Vicious circles,' Kierkegaard called them, vicious circles, when the quality of life is subordinated to abstractions and morality forced to give way to rationality. Do you understand that if economic usefulness is the only measure of the choices we have to make as a society, then we are at the mercy of excess? Because numbers can never be big enough. And that's the only real reason why our society is now so chaotic. We stray in all directions, driven by and delivered up to our own anxieties and desires.

"Science as ideology has made us not just stupid but mute. We no longer have any idea of the meaning of words, and we've become incapable of carrying on a real conversation. What remains is chatter. And the biggest chatterers are the people who have most to say: politicians, business people, media personalities. But all right, this morning Good News was proclaimed, the immortal machine-human will be born, a star is shining in the west of the West. Be that as it may, I'd rather be a mortal man with a heart and a soul than an immortal but soulless human-machine. I'd rather live in a humanist civilization with a moral order that will always have to be fought for in the face of barbaric forces than be submerged in a world full of science and technology. I had hoped this science horror was science fiction. I regret having to learn this morning that that's not so, and I regret even more that all this is welcomed, heartily and brainlessly, by you."

That last remark, after what was already quite a tirade, was a slap in the face to all those who had loudly applauded Shashi's vision, and I felt

Walter would have done better not to have said it. Even polite applause was now no longer possible, and Wolfgang was plainly unhappy with the whole situation. To break the painful silence, he said, "Well, Walter, that's truly a lot of food for thought. Fortunately, there's also a lot of food for the body, so let's have lunch!"

Not even looking at Walter, Shashi picked up his things and left the library without a word. The others followed.

It struck me that Radim, the elderly Czech who had seemed so absent while Shashi was speaking, had listened attentively to Walter, and when the others left, he went over to him and silently but emphatically shook his hand. Jossi came over to Walter as well and remarked, "Thanks, Walter. I'm very happy with what you said." I believe Walter's eyes grew a little damp when it became clear he wasn't alone.

After lunch I took a walk and made some notes for tomorrow. With any luck the weather will improve and the sun will put everyone in a better mood.

Friday

The peace here is so benevolent, the air so pure, that I slept well and rose early to take a short morning walk before breakfast. Everything smells of autumn. Wisps of fog lie over the meadows, but the mountaintops are already clear. This place, surrounded by so much natural beauty, has something otherworldly about it. It's as if the noise and ugliness of the world are excluded.

In the breakfast room I found Wolfgang, who told me about an argument between Shashi and Walter yesterday. Shashi felt insulted at being called "brainless" (and that certainly won't have been the only thing) and demanded an apology. Walter refused, observing that Shashi shouldn't take what he'd said so literally and that if symposia could no longer be the setting for a critical exchange of views, we might just as well go to church and obediently listen to Good News stories, and he had no need of that. Wolfgang managed to calm things down by getting Walter to explain to Shashi that his criticism concerned his ideas and didn't indicate anything less than full respect for him as a person. Wolfgang immediately had a bottle of wine brought in to celebrate this "peace."

We talked for a moment about why he continues to organize these symposia. He said, "We can complain endlessly about the world of power, politicians, business people, and so on, but the way the world is, what we find important and what we believe in are things determined by the world of ideas, which is where intellectuals have the most influence, so we need this intellectual debate and I invite them here, even if they're not always the most pleasant of company." He had to laugh at that.

It seemed news had spread throughout the hotel that the symposium was anything but dull, since extra chairs had to be brought to the library to accommodate a far bigger audience. Because there were so many new people, I began my introductory remarks about the importance of democracy with a reference to something Walter said yesterday: "We live in a time without yardsticks, society is directionless and driven by irrational fears and desires, and this is all because of the dominance of scientific truth—which can determine facts but not meaning; which knows about quantity but not what quality means—and we have lost metaphysical truth."

I explained that Nietzsche understood this too and came to the same conclusion: without universal and absolute truth, without God or Logos or objective reason—or whatever you want to call the domain of spiritual values—there are no longer any social criteria for what is truly of value, what is just, what makes human existence decent. This loss, Nietzsche said, will sweep away the foundations of our civilization, and what remains is nihilism: submission to excess. No longer do we have the ambition to attain a higher life, to make our own everything that will enable us to rise above the bestial, which is also part of our nature; instead we want the opposite, with our incessant desire for quantity, for mass, our endless intoxication, that insatiable hunger for more, more, more.

Robert Musil, the engineer and writer famous for his 1930s novel *The Man Without Qualities*, woke from an intellectual sleep, along with others of his generation, when the First World War ended. Suddenly they realized that the world had changed drastically. Before the war, they'd believed in humanism and art; there had been a shared awareness of good and evil. After that war, they realized that humanism had gone, and they found themselves in a technological era they could never have imagined, with no idea how the world ought to go on from there.

Before he published *The Man Without Qualities*, Musil wrote, "Each era must have a guideline, a raison d'être, a balance between theory and ethics, God etc. As yet, the Age of Empiricism has failed." He hoped to offer that guideline in his novel, to formulate what the (new?) yardstick ought to be. But the novel remained unfinished. As an engineer, Musil was a friend and admirer of science and technology, but as a writer, he knew that science and technology would never be able to offer such yardsticks. Others think differently on the subject, even now—and I looked at Shashi, but he was looking around, bored— but the criticism expressed by Walter yesterday was expressed in a different way by the famous cultural psychologist Erich Fromm.

In 1968 Fromm published *The Revolution of Hope*, in which he wrote,

A specter is stalking in our midst whom only a few see with clarity. It is not the old ghost of communism or fascism. It is a new specter: a completely mechanized society, devoted to maximal material output and consumption, directed by computers; and in this social process, man himself is being transformed into a part of the total machine, well fed and entertained, yet passive, unalive, and with little feeling. With the victory of the new society, individualism and privacy will have disappeared; feelings toward others will be engineered by psychological conditioning and other devices, or drugs which also serve a new kind of introspective experience.

Even Shashi no longer looked bored when I read out that quote. I followed it up by saying that I did not want to speak any further about science and technology now but instead about a different "guideline," which after the Second World War became the guideline for the Western world: democracy. After the nightmare of totalitarianism, the realization dawned in Europe that there can be freedom only if there is also democracy. The Americans had realized this back in 1776. For the old world, it was a belated echo of what Spinoza stated in 1670 in his *Tractatus Theologico-Politicus*: "The true aim of government is liberty." There was some hilarity when I said that three pages further on Spinoza wrote, "He who seeks to regulate everything by law, is more likely to arouse vices than to reform them." I added that these wise words have unfortunately been forgotten both in Brussels and in Washington. But what is democracy? And is democracy indeed the guarantee that we can live in freedom?

Since those present were mostly Americans and Europeans, I chose to tell them what a European, Thomas Mann, had to say to an American audience about democracy. It was in 1938, when he was already an admirer and friend of President Franklin Roosevelt, and he spoke about "The Coming Victory of Democracy" at fifteen different places, often in front of thousands of people, in a coast-to-coast lecture tour. In his lecture, Mann defined democracy as "that form of government and of society which is inspired above every other with the feeling and conscious-ness of the dignity of man."

These are big words, and Mann was well aware how petty people could be with their ego-tism, cruelty, cowardice, and stupidity. Precisely for that reason we must never forget that "the great and honorable in man manifest themselves as art and science, a passion for truth, creation of beauty, and the idea of justice." These are the things a democracy, a true democracy, will cul-tivate, because democracy is the form of govern-ment that attempts to elevate human beings, to enable them to think and to be free. The goal of democracy is therefore education, intellec-tual development, and nobility of spirit, and nobility of spirit is the most important weapon against the degeneration of democracy into mass democracy, whereby demagogues, stupidity, pro-paganda, claptrap, vulgarity, and the lowest of human instincts increase their dominance until they inevitably give birth to the bastard child of democracy: fascism.

I added that less than two years later, in Los Angeles, Mann addressed his audience in a lecture entitled "War and Democracy" with the following words: "Let me tell you the whole truth: if ever fascism should come to America, it will come in the name of freedom."

All this seemed to me sufficient to enable the symposium to become a real conversation and to ask whether the participants thought Western civilization, eager as it is to divide the world into good (democracy) and evil (no democracy), is itself at this point a democracy or a mass democracy? The answer would be important in attempting to understand how we will deal with current technological developments. Do we have a grip on those developments, or is technology gaining a grip on us? We can assume that in a democracy people keep a grip on their own existence. In a mass democracy, by contrast, everyone is in the grip of anything that can cast a spell on the masses.

I was rather shocked that almost all those present, including quite a few of the Americans, were of the opinion that we have arrived at a mass democracy and that the future may be far less rosy than was assumed a generation ago. Roger, a lawyer from New York, dressed for the past two days in a suit and bow tie, said he had been inspired by the work of Hannah Arendt and that, bearing in mind her analysis of society, he could see unmistakable fascistic tendencies once more, even in the United States. Speaking directly to Shashi, he went on, "Our technological ingenuity cannot conceal intellectual emptiness and spiritual poverty, Shashi. Our universities teach above all how to earn money, not how to think for ourselves. Walter was right yesterday: our society, especially in America, is being made increasingly stupid. So yes, there is plenty of space for new demagogues, xenophobia, the politics of fear, and nationalism. We see it everywhere, there's no denying it."

Andrew, who worked for a Republican senator, produced a quote from John Adams, the second U.S. president, who warned in a letter to the political philosopher John Taylor in 1814: "Remember, democracy never lasts long. It soon wastes, exhausts and murders itself. There never was a democracy yet that did not commit suicide." Precisely the fact that this was written two hundred years ago and that in those two centuries America has not fallen into the trap of fascism is sufficient reason, Andrew said, not to worry too much now. He observed cheerfully, "Eventually, we Americans always do the right thing." That remark naturally led to a great deal of debate, but the consensus was that not even America is immune to the bacillus known as fascism. Iso, a Swiss, who calls himself *ein freischwebender Intellektueller*, a free-floating intellectual, remarked sarcastically that we'd do better not to talk about his country and the rest of the West. Here, Iso said, the lessons of history have not been learned. Fascism is raising its head again everywhere, in a new, modern guise. We like to deny the fact by calling it "populism," but it is so obvious that it would be a waste of time to talk about it any further.

Then Maricruz, a Spanish student of political

science, asked the question that is always asked: "But what can we do?"

I answered that it would be good to ask ourselves, before thinking about that question, why so little was being done to oppose the returning ghosts, which after the Second World War were thought to be disappearing for good. What is the role, the responsibility of the elites in our society?

I pointed out that Walter said something important yesterday in this regard. We have lost an awareness of *quality* and now believe only in *quantity*, just as Nietzsche predicted when he wrote of the power of the "greatest number." Which elites, I asked, are dominant in our democracy? They are the financial, political, military, media, and sporting elites. These are all characterized by the quantity they represent: the most power, the greatest influence, the most money, the greatest strength, and the most prizes. In the cultural world, the concept of an elite has a fundamentally different meaning. The *best* artist is not the artist who earns the most money or sells the most work or attracts the most attention, but rather the artist whose work will bear the test of time and still speak to an audience several hundred years from now. The best intellectual or thinker is not the one most often featured in the media, who writes lots of newspaper articles and is regarded as an opinion-former, but rather the one whose work will endure.

In the world of culture, *elite* refers to quality, not quantity. The fact that the true intellectual and artistic elites are now marginalized almost everywhere in the Western world, while power elites are more dominant than ever, is reflected in the values cultivated, values that are a perfect reflection of commerce, technology, and kitsch and are completely unrelated to Thomas Mann's description of "the great and honorable in humanity, which manifest themselves as art and science, as passion for truth, creation of beauty, and the idea of justice." We should therefore expect no changes from power elites. They constitute the power, they have the power, because their worldview represents the expression of a society as it now is. If society changes, they lose their power. Only in exceptional cases do you find in the world of power a few who have the courage to be different, who have an ideal to live by, who are capable of clearly formulating the guideline for a better world that Musil sought and of embedding it in action.

The conclusion can only be that the power elites are themselves the crisis. Through what they think and do, they are the incarnation of all those values that make true democracy impossible in our time. Not because they are bad people. That's not the point. They simply don't know any better. They adapt in order to keep their jobs and to belong, they are too busy to think properly, and they truly believe that what they do is for the best because it fits their worldview—a worldview they long ago became incapable of looking at critically, because they no longer dare to look at themselves in the mirror.

So what can we do? In his speech about democracy, Thomas Mann claimed that education is the heart of democracy. This is remarkable because for us democracy is always measured by freedom and suffrage, freedom of expression, the rule of law, and human rights. Mann would not deny this, but he points to a pillar of democracy that reaches much further: education. The question, of course, is: *Education in what?* Because, as Musil already knew, that era of humanism is over. Education in what? What can become a yardstick for us again, a different yardstick from that of the market or power, which merely speculate upon our most primitive instincts? Where do we find the guideline, Ariadne's thread, that can lead us back to a decent, civilized society if we decide after all not to opt for the "human-machine society"?

Radim, the elderly Czech, whom I believed Wolfgang had invited only because he was a friend of Václav Havel, the man who sat in silence reading a book for two days, more absent than present—it was he who to everyone's surprise remarked laconically in response to my question, "I do have an idea. But if you don't mind, I'm now going to smoke my cigar, and I'll tell it to you tomorrow." He took his book in his left hand, in the other the stick without which he could no longer walk, and was the first to leave the library, coughing and breathing heavily. *That cigar,* I thought, *that cigar is not a good idea, Radim. It'll kill you.*

I didn't do much for the rest of the day, just walked a little and read Nietzsche's *Letters* in the sun. I was glad my job here was finished, and I was very curious about what Radim would have to say tomorrow, because I was not much the wiser about the return of Europa. No, that's not true, I believed I did now know the answer to the question Mann asked at the time of the rise of the Hitler regime: "Are the European, classical values timeless and universal, or are they temporary and tied to an episode in the history of humanity?" Based on everything I had seen and heard in Sils-Maria and now here, I feared that the answer could only be that Princess Europa would not return.

That would mean remaining vigilant, reading, writing long letters. . . .

Saturday
Wolfgang said it was serendipity, a happy coincidence, that I rang him when he was looking for a speaker on the subject of democracy. If that was

the case, then it was far more serendipitous that I had the opportunity to meet Radim here. On the final morning of the symposium, I learned a great deal more about Europe from him than in all my years of study. I didn't know him, had never even heard of him, partly because, as I now discover to my amazement, he's never written a book!

To my shame, I also have to admit that I expected little out of the ordinary from him because of his physical appearance. Old age had caused him to shrink, a hump in his back made him even smaller, his nails were uncut, hairs poked at least a centimeter out of his nostrils, and his clothes smelled as if they saw a washing machine no more than once a month. He kept himself to himself, not trying to make contact, and over the past few days he'd been reading a book, preferably alone. One of us was struck by the fact that he was reading Kafka and asked in surprise why he had only now got around to the work of his famous fellow townsman. "Young man," Radim said in a friendly voice, "it's not 'only now' but 'once again,' the reason being that every time I read Kafka's work, I learn some-thing new. And Kafka has far more to tell me than any number of my fellow men. Enjoy your walk." And the man who had asked, no longer knowing what to say, simply walked on.

It remains astonishing, the experience that your judgment is merely a prejudice that, like all prejudices, is no more substantial than a big lump of chocolate that melts in the burning sun and drips away. This Radim, this unsightly lit-tle man with his 1950s spectacles and wrecked lungs, knew something about Europe unknown to all of Brussels and to all European experts, something that would probably never be under-stood. If it were, then Prague would become the capital of a United Europe. Brussels never can be, because . . . That is how Radim's story began, the true story of Europe. I took it down verba-tim, so I would never forget it:

"Every place on earth has its genius loci: the spirit of place that determines its nature. The fact that the EU organization has its seat in giant office buildings as characterless as they are ugly, and what's more in a city that has played no appreciable part in the history of the West, says a great deal about this union that calls itself European. Your birthplace is a result of happenstance. At least, I assume it is. It's therefore not a merit, and so I think myself all the more fortunate, despite the painful fate of my country in the accursed twentieth century, to have been born in 1930 in Prague.

"Anyone who has been there will know that it's one of the most beautiful cities in Europe. For lovers of literature, it's the city of Kafka, Max Brod, and Milena Jesenská; for musicians the city of Dvořák and Smetana and the place where Mozart's *Don Giovanni* had its premiere; for astronomers, it's the city of David Gans and where Tycho Brahe and Kepler worked; for Jews, the city of Rabbi Jehudi Löw; for theologians, the city of Jan Hus; for educationalists, the city of Comenius; political scientists will think of Masaryk and my friend Havel; and a few historians will still know that in 1356 Petrarch went to visit his friend Emperor Charles IV there. All true Europeans will know their cultural history and therefore most of these familiar facts.

"Yet this knowledge is not what makes a European a European. What does that is something that I was privileged to learn from a man who is no less than a Socrates of our time. Was. He is dead. Killed. Just like Socrates. Not by a cup of poison but by exhaustion, the torture of a sick man of almost seventy, who was interrogated relentlessly by the Prague Communist regime until he collapsed. He was hated by them because he spoke the truth and taught us, his pupils— although he wouldn't let us call ourselves that— to live in truth.

"Jan Patočka was his name. You don't know him. That is the fate of people who don't set out to achieve fame. Havel, whom you do know, and I, we were among his students. Those in power banned Patočka from teaching at the university, and so we, actually just like you here, usually gathered in an attic room. We drank tea, with lots of sugar if there was any, and listened to what Patočka had to teach us. He had no books, no materials. He told us what he knew, what he'd come to understand, and what we too must know and try to understand in order to be European.

"After Patočka died on March 13, 1977, Václav quite rightly wrote, and I quote, 'The power of Patočka resided not only in his great erudition and ability to think but in his openness, modesty, and humor. At attic meetings he enabled us to experience what philosophy is in the original meaning of the word: not classroom boredom, but rather the inspired, vital search for the significance of things and the illumination of understanding one's own situation in the world.' Václav wrote beautifully; he could express so much so well. After Patočka was taken from us, we put all our notes together to record his words, what he had taught us about Europe, in a single book.

"What is Europe? Who is the European, *Homo europaeus*? Europe, Patočka told us, is born out of care for the soul. That is also what defines Europeans: *care for the soul*. Every evening he urged us never to forget this, because the future of the West is contained in it. If we should ever stop caring about the soul, Europe would cease to exist. I see rather pitying looks on several of your faces. I'll explain what Patočka meant.

"Every person, at least those who are not yet

human-machines, is a moral being, which is to say a being in search of meaning, who wants to know what things are good and what things are evil, what is of value and what is not, and what is the truth and the purpose of human existence. That knowledge, knowledge of the moral order, was once founded in the existence of God, then in nature, and after that in reason—our own rationality would be able to tell us the meaning of life. After the loss of our faith in God, we started to believe in progress, because the future would solve all our problems. But before long it turned out that nature does not guide progress. And reason, to which the Enlightenment attached so much value, could not promise us progress either.

"But science could! Technology could! They offered us demonstrable progress. At least, so we thought. It soon transpired that technical rationality, mechanical thinking, is completely without meaning. Logic, mathematics, technology: these things know nothing of value, meaning, ethics. A teacher of Patočka's, the philosopher Husserl, was the first to realize that our rationality was in crisis. Technological, instrumental rationality, which has no knowledge of good and evil or of what makes life meaningful, was the essence of the crisis of our time. Because a philosophy, a way of thinking that cannot show us any meaning, that therefore cannot offer us guidance or a yardstick, creates plenty of space for the irrational, including the insane political passions of nationalism, anti-Semitism, racism, and fascism. Husserl was convinced that since the European crisis was rooted in a rationalism gone awry, Europe faced a choice between rebirth from the spirit of true philosophy or barbarism.

"Walter made a few important observations the day before yesterday about the consequences of a truth that is allowed to be merely scientific and rational. I'm grateful to him for that. I also agree with him that today's universities, institutions traditionally intended to cultivate the European spirit, are now, in their obsession with economics and technology, focused mainly on the destruction of the European spirit and therefore only contribute to the deep crisis of civilization in which we find ourselves.

"For Patočka, who experienced that barbarism personally, the betrayal of Munich in 1938, when Western Europe chose to allow political self-interest to prevail over the defense of European values, always remained a trauma. At that moment he knew that politics, the world of power, would never defend the European spirit. The world of power is interested only in power, power and property. Not in freedom, not in justice, not in the European soul. And as long as that remains the case, history will continue to repeat itself on this continent. An eternal return of bloodletting. Statesmen like Masaryk, Roosevelt, and Churchill were the great exceptions. That was why they were statesmen. An exceptional breed. Patočka knew that, and so he saw it as his task to rediscover the spirit of true philosophy and educate us about it. He started to read Plato, and Plato became his teacher, his Virgil in the search for the soul of Europe.

"The first thing he learned from Plato was that true philosophy is *meta*physics. It is philosophy that surpasses empiricism, the everyday world, because it tries to understand the deeper significance of being human. That is what makes European culture unique. Europe is not a tradition of customs passed down—no, Europe is first of all that quest for true humanity. What is the essence of the human being? Well, this is what Socrates stressed in almost all his conversations: it is the soul, the immortal soul, that makes a human being human. By virtue of their possession of a soul, human beings are the only creatures fully aware of their own vulnerability, their mortality. That is the fundamental anxiety felt by every man or woman. At the same time, we have our souls to thank for our greatness, because our souls enable us to know the absolute, the eternal, that which is not transitory: truth, goodness, beauty, love, and justice. *Ecce homo.*

"The greatness of human beings is their ability to make these spiritual values, which are eternal, their own in time. That is also the aim of every great artist: to allow us to experience this imperishable world. Kafka, a native of Prague like me, noted this desire in his diary: 'I can derive temporary satisfaction from works like *A Country Doctor,* assuming they are successful (very improbably). But happiness comes to me only when I can elevate the world into the realm of the pure, true and immutable.' Before him, Walt Whitman, the American who was such a European soul, wrote in his immortal *Leaves of Grass*: 'And I have dream'd that the purpose and essence of the known life, the transient, is to form and decide identity for the unknown life, the permanent.'

"Even earlier, Dante expressed the essence of his art and existence in his Inferno as something he learned from his teacher Brunetto Latini: *M'insegnavate come l'uom s'etterna.* 'You taught me how man makes himself eternal.'

"So the language of the poet, the language of the Muses, is one of the most important gifts given to us. It is the language in which we learn to know the Logos, the meaning of those spiritual values, as expressed in words. The chatter of the media, the hot air of politicians, the sales talk of commerce, the hollow jargon of academics, it all, literally and figuratively, says nothing. For it is meaningless.

"Care for the soul, the ability to give the eternal a place in time—that is what philosophy is. It gives all of us the ability to rise above ourselves, to be our better selves, to change ourselves, and to give truth and justice a home in this world. The essence of Europe is therefore never politics, nor economics, nor technology, no, it is culture. Nothing else. It is no accident that our concept of culture stems from Cicero's statement *Cultura animi, filosofia est.* 'The cultivation of the soul— that is philosophy.' Wise words, taught to him by Socrates, and all true Europeans have these words engraved in their hearts. For the sake of that cultivation of the soul, for the sake of the continual search for those spiritual values and the endeavor to make them our own, for the sake of all these things, any philosophy worthy of the name is always metaphysics. Philosophy can never be a doctrine or an ideology, because the good, the beautiful, and the true can never be captured in a single form. This search, this care for the soul, this endeavor to live in truth and to make the world just, will never be completed. Which means that being a European is above all a state of mind, and Europe is never completed.

"To be a European also means to *fight*, to fight for a European humanist society in which not the individual but the idea of the human being is central, with education—above all, universities— where young people can make a cultural-moral consciousness their own, where the human soul is cultivated so that people become morally mature and are led in their society by a desire for truth and justice. Because only this, care for the soul—the desire of the soul to be fed by truth and justice and to live in a true and just world— only that can be the yardstick, the guideline for a world that wants to be civilized.

"But look at the reality! *Ecce mundus*. See why Patočka was murdered, is known by no one in our own time, and if he were alive today, he'd be totally ignored and certainly not given a position at a university. I don't know whether you have ever had the opportunity to read *The Trial* by my beloved Kafka. At one point in that novel K., the nameless central character, comes upon a priest in the cathedral who, after everything K. has been through, talks nonsense to him, since he appeals to all that is useful, necessary, and K.

responds by saying, 'The lie made into the rule of the world.'

"That, to my great sorrow, is what the EU has done. That Union that calls itself European is nothing other than an Economic Union, where the terms *soul, culture, philosophy,* and *live in truth* are as impossible as a palm tree on the moon. By denying the spiritual foundation, the soul of Europe, and by ignoring culture, philosophy, and art with boundless arrogance in favor of economics, technology, and national interests, by cultivating a bureaucracy and diplomacy that can think and act only according to economic interests and political values—and even the latter only to a very small degree—we have allowed a lie to rule the Union that makes us forget the true greatness of humankind. Instead of the cultivation of the soul, we see the rebirth of nationalism, the triviality of technology, the vulgarity of commerce, and the cultivated stupidity of the media and the universities.

"Patočka told us time and again that we stand before a choice that for a long time has concerned not only our hemisphere but the whole of planet Earth and the future of humanity. Will we accept the return of barbarism, or will we fight for the rebirth of nobility of spirit? I am old, dear people. My body is used up, and I will not live much longer. The choice is yours. It ought to be easy to make, but my time has taught me how difficult this choice is, because most people are simply not combative and brave."

It was very quiet when Radim finished speaking. By the time someone finally dared to say something, he had left the library with his walking stick. I felt as if I'd seen a ghost: the ghost of Socrates.

Sunday

It's now afternoon, and soon I too will be leaving this place I love so much, this time to return to the lowlands. Last night I slept badly. I kept thinking about the story—more of a lecture, really—told by Radim. After breakfast I packed my suitcase, and because it's now a beautiful autumn day here, I decided to take one more walk, first through the woods and then past the meadow back to the hotel. When I got to the woods, I saw ahead of me a small, bent little man in an oversize coat, walking slowly with a stick. It could only be Radim. I quickly walked over to him, and when he recognized me, he said: "Come on, young man, give me your arm. With a little more support it's easier for me to walk, or were you planning on a long hike? In that case, I don't want to hold you up." I gave him my arm and said I merely wanted to walk a little before leaving and that I was hugely grateful to him for everything he said yesterday.

"Good," he said. "Then at least there's one person who really wanted to listen."

"I don't think I'm the only one, Radim."

"It doesn't matter all that much. Come on, there's a seat. I can rest for a moment and light a cigar."

"Is that sensible?"

"Dear boy, I'm an old man and I don't have long to live, but as long as I'm here, I want to enjoy all the beauty of the earth and the pleasures of life." He lit his beloved cigar and asked, "Why did you come to this symposium?"

I told him about my search for Princess Europa and the question of whether she could ever return. About how by chance I had gone to Sils-Maria, to Grand Hotel Waldhaus, and about everything I saw and heard there: the priest who wanted to entrust mastery of the world to his Church, my walk past the house where Anne Frank played in her holidays, the memory of Paul Celan . . .

"I'm very glad, Radim, that I came upon you here. Very glad. You have given me courage again, and now I dare to believe once more that Europa can return, even if, as you said yourself, it will not be easy."

With his small, glistening eyes behind his far from fashionable spectacles and with a smile on his wrinkled face, he said, "Ah, Europa, that beautiful and brave princess. She can certainly return, but then you'll have to tell her story. Europa is a story full of tears but also of great deeds and an undying dream. Come on, we're leaving. You have to go home to tell a story. I've an idea it will be a whole book."

ABOUT THE AUTHOR

ROB RIEMEN is the author of *Nobility of Spirit: A Forgotten Ideal* (2008), which was translated into eighteen languages. A writer and cultural philosopher, he is also the president of the Nexus Institute, which he founded in 1994. With the institute, in the tradition of European humanism, Riemen publishes the journal *Nexus* and organizes Nexus lectures, seminars, symposia, and conferences in Amsterdam with the world's foremost intellectuals, artists, diplomats, politicians, and other decision makers, to inspire public intellectual debate about the most important subjects for humanity and society. He lives in the Netherlands.